LawExpress
INTELLECTUAL
PROPERTY LAW

INTELLECTUAL PROPERTY LAW

Law Express

4th edition

David Bainbridge
Aston University

Claire Howell
Aston University

Harlow, England • London • New York • Boston • San Francisco • Toronto • Sydney • Auckland • Singapore • Hong Kong
Tokyo • Seoul • Taipei • New Delhi • Cape Town • São Paulo • Mexico City • Madrid • Amsterdam • Munich • Paris • Milan

Pearson Education Limited
Edinburgh Gate
Harlow CM20 2JE
United Kingdom
Tel: +44 (0)1279 623623
Web: www.pearson.com/uk

First published 2009 (print and electronic)
Second edition published 2011 (print and electronic)
Third edition published 2013 (print and electronic)
Fourth edition published 2015 (print and electronic)

Contains public sector information licensed under the Open Government Licence (OGL) v2.0.
www.nationalarchives.gov.uk/doc/open-government-licence.

Pearson Education is not responsible for the content of third-party internet sites.

ISBN: 978-1-292-01278-0 (print)
      978-1-292-01352-7 (PDF)
      978-1-292-01799-0 (ePub)
      978-1-292-01296-4 (eText)

British Library Cataloguing-in-Publication Data
A catalogue record for the print edition is available from the British Library

Library of Congress Cataloging-in-Publication Data
Bainbridge, David I., author.
   Intellectual property law / David Bainbridge; Claire Howell, Aston University. -- 4th edition.
     pages cm. -- (Law express)
   Includes bibliographical references and index.
   ISBN 978-1-292-01278-0
   1. Intellectual property--Great Britain--Outlines, syllabi, etc.   I. Howell, Claire, author.   II. Title.
   KD1269.B356 2014
   346.4104'8--dc23
                        2014009447

ARP impression 98

Print edition typeset in 10/12pt Helvetica Neue LT Std by 35
Print edition printed and bound in Great Britain by Ashford Colour Press Ltd

NOTE THAT ANY PAGE CROSS REFERENCES REFER TO THE PRINT EDITION

Contents

Supporting resources

Visit the *Law Express* series companion website at **www.pearsoned.co.uk/lawexpress** to find valuable student learning material including:

- A **study plan** test to help you assess how well you know the subject before you begin your revision.
- Interactive **quizzes** to test your knowledge of the main points from each chapter.
- Sample **examination questions** and guidelines for answering them.
- Interactive **flashcards** to help you revise key terms, cases and statutes.
- Printable versions of the **topic maps** and **checklists** from the book.
- **'You be the marker'** allows you to see exam questions and answers from the perspective of the examiner and includes notes on how an answer might be marked.
- **Podcasts** provide point-by-point instruction on how to answer a typical exam question.

Also: The companion website provides the following features:

- Search tool to help locate specific items of content
- E-mail results and profile tools to send results of quizzes to instructors
- Online help and support to assist with website usage and troubleshooting

For more information please contact your local Pearson Education sales representative or visit **www.pearsoned.co.uk/lawexpress**

Acknowledgements

Our thanks go to all reviewers who contributed to the development of this text, including students who participated in research and focus groups which helped to shape the series format.

Introduction

Intellectual property law is a demanding but rewarding and enjoyable subject. It covers a range of diverse rights, some of which have little in common with others. Students should keep in mind that, although some rights may be quite different from others, a number of rights may exist in respect of the same subject-matter. For example, a new design of plastic bottle for tomato ketchup may be protected by design law (registered and unregistered), trade mark law and the law of passing off. The label attached to the bottle may be protected by artistic and literary copyright. Students are likely to get extra marks if they can demonstrate that they understand the overlap between the different intellectual property rights.

This book is a revision guide. It is intended to help focus students on the key areas in which they are likely to be examined. It also acts as an aide mémoire, picking out key cases and statutes. It is no substitute for textbooks and other materials with which students should be familiar. Students should also be aware that this revision guide cannot cover all the ground which may be covered in a module on intellectual property. For example, it has not been possible to cover areas such rights in performances.

Students should frequently check the syllabus of the module they are taking and refer to lecture notes, handouts and virtual learning materials provided by their lecturer and module leader. As intellectual property is such a big subject, most lecturers are likely to concentrate on some parts of the subject and deal with others in less detail. By reviewing the content of the course as taught or given as directed learning, students will have a much better idea of the areas they are likely to be examined on. Past examination papers also provide a rich form of guidance but students must be aware that, in a fast-moving subject like intellectual property, older examination questions may have been overtaken by recent developments. Questions in past examination papers should be attempted, provided they have current relevance. Ideally, students should attempt past examination questions after getting to grips with the subject area. Allow the time permitted in the examination and go through your answers critically, seeing how they could be improved (You be the Marker section on the companion website gives guidance on this).

Inevitably, during the teaching of a module, there will be legislative changes to and/or important cases on intellectual property law. Examiners are impressed with students who show that they have taken the trouble to look up and understand the latest developments. Students should also be reminded that it is well worth reading the judgments in important

Supreme Court (formerly House of Lords), Court of Appeal and Patents Court cases and rulings of the Court of Justice of the European Union. Read and discuss other materials you are directed to by your lecturer, such as articles from specialised intellectual property journals.

Bear in mind the justifications for intellectual property rights (IPR). By granting limited rights, whether or not monopoly rights, innovation and investment into creating new works and inventions is stimulated. This results in increased employment, wealth and research and development into the creation of new technologies and improvements thereto. IPR are particularly important in the development of new pharmaceuticals and biotechnological inventions. Another justification is that the subject-matter of IPR results from the exercise of human intellect, and a person should not be deprived of it without fair compensation by granting him or her rights over it limited in time and scope.

📖 REVISION NOTE

Things to bear in mind when revising intellectual property law:

- Problem questions can be quite complex and it might be worthwhile drawing a 'mind map' or making a list of relevant dates before attempting the question. Spend a little time ensuring that you understand the question.

- Essay questions often require students to consider policy issues or unsatisfactory areas such as patents for computer-implemented inventions.

- Exam questions are not an excuse to write down everything you know about a particular area – answer what the question asks, not what you wished it had asked.

- Make full use of the recommended textbooks and other materials your lecturer suggests. Do not rely on this revision guide to learn the subject.

- Make sure you understand the main legislative provisions dealing with matters such as subsistence, requirements for registration and exceptions, authors, designers, inventors, ownership and entitlement, duration, infringement and defences.

- Seek advice from your lecturer about what you should revise. Most lecturers are very happy to give advice, guidance and feedback.

- Do not 'cherry-pick', only revising part of the syllabus. Questions on intellectual property often cover a wide range and may include a number of different and disparate intellectual property rights. Only omit revising a particular part of the syllabus if your lecturer has expressly confirmed that it will not be examined.

- Attempt past exam questions and review how your answer could be improved. Some lecturers are happy to look at your attempts and give you feedback. But make sure you do not waste time attempting past examination questions that are no longer relevant because of changes in the law.

Before you begin, you can use the study plan available on the companion website to assess how well you know the material in this book and identify the areas where you may want to focus your revision.

Guided tour

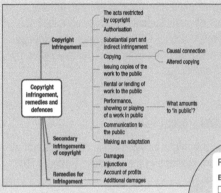

Topic maps – Visual guides highlight key subject areas and facilitate easy navigation through the chapter. Download them from the companion website to pin on your wall or add to your revision notes.

Revision checklists – How well do you know each topic? Use these to identify essential points you should know for your exams. But don't panic if you don't know them all – the chapters will help you revise each point to ensure you are fully prepared. Print the checklists off the companion website and track your revision progress!

Revision checklist

Essential points you should kno

- [ ] The acts restricted by copyright
- [ ] What amounts to copying and the con
- [ ] Secondary infringements of copyright
- [ ] Remedies for infringement of copyri
- [ ] Assessment of damages
- [ ] Injunctions against service prov
- [ ] The Digital Economy Act 20
- [ ] Defences to copyrigh

Sample questions with answer guidelines – Practice makes perfect! Read the question at the start of each chapter and consider how you would answer it. Guidance on structuring strong answers is provided at the end of the chapter. Try out additional sample questions online.

Sample question

Could you answer this question? Below is a typical essay question that could arise on this topic. Guidelines on answering the question are included at the end of this chapter, whilst a sample problem question and guidance on tackling it can be found on the companion website.

Assessment advice – Not sure how best to tackle a problem or essay question? Wondering what you may be asked? Use the assessment advice to identify the ways in which a subject may be examined and how to apply your knowledge effectively.

ASSESSMENT ADVICE

Essay questions

You may be asked to discuss the difficulty in establishing what is a substantial amount of a work for infringement purposes. Alternatively, the balance between protecting the author of a work and the need for freedom of expression in relation to the fair dealing defences may also be a possible question.

Problem questions

This is a prime area for problem questions. A scenario where there has been some conscious or unconscious infringement, possibly an adaptation or, alternatively, altered

Key definitions – Make sure you understand essential legal terms. Use the flashcards online to test your recall!

KEY DEFINITION: Authorise

To 'authorise' means to grant or purport to grant to a third person the right to do the act complained of.

Key cases and key statutes – Identify and review the important elements of the essential cases and statutes you will need to know for your exams.

KEY CASE

CBS Songs Ltd v Amstrad Consumer Electronics plc [1988] 1 AC 1013, HL

Concerning: whether providing machines which could be used for copyright infringement was authorising infringement

Facts

Amstrad was held not to be authorising copyright infringement by the sale of its twin-deck tape recorder machines which could be used to copy music, thereby infringing its copyright.

Make your answer stand out – This feature illustrates sources of further thinking and debate where you can maximise your marks. Use them to really impress your examiners!

✓   Make your answer stand out

The idea/expression debate is a long-standing one in the field of copyright. Ronan Deazley (2004) considers two House of Lords cases on what constitutes a substantial part. Make your answer stand out by explaining that Deazley discusses the idea/expression debate and asks whether the balance is weighted too much in favour of the author with the potential that creativity by others will be inhibited.

Exam tips – Feeling the pressure? These boxes indicate how you can improve your exam performance when it really counts.

EXAM TIP

Point out that if the courts concentrate on quality to determine substantiality they may end up demanding merit of the copyright work, and for original works no merit is required.

Revision notes – Get guidance for effective revision. These boxes highlight related points and areas of overlap in the subject, or areas where your course might adopt a particular approach that you should check with your course tutor.

REVISION NOTE

See Chapter 1 for discussion of adaptation of musical works and *Hyperion Records* v *Sawkins.*

Don't be tempted to . . . – This feature underlines areas where students most often trip up in exams. Use them to spot common pitfalls and avoid losing marks.

!   Don't be tempted to . . .

Don't forget that when determining infringement by taking a substantial part, the method is to first identify the parts taken by the defendant, *then* isolate them from the remainder of the defendant's work, and *only then* consider whether those parts represent a substantial part of the claimant's work (*not the defendant's work*).

Read to impress – Focus on these carefully selected sources to extend your knowledge, deepen your understanding, and earn better marks in coursework as well as in exams.

READ TO IMPRESS

Deazley, R. (2004) 'Copyright in the House of Lords: recent cases, juridical reasoning and academic writing', 2 *Intellectual Property Quarterly*, 121.

Derclaye, E. (2010) '*Infopaq International A/S v Danske Dagblades Forening* (C-5/08): wonderful or worrisome? The impact of the ECJ ruling in *Infopaq* on UK copyright law', 32(5) *EIPR* 247.

Heath-Saunders, A. (2005) 'It's a fair copy: the defence of fair dealing in cases of copyright infringement', June, *Corporate Briefing* 8.

Rahmatian, A. (2012) *Temple Island Collections* v *New English Teas* 34(11) *EIPR* 796

Glossary – Forgotten the meaning of a word? This quick reference covers key definitions and other useful terms.

Glossary of terms

The glossary is divided into two parts: key definitions and other useful terms. The key definitions can be found within the chapter in which they occur as well as in the glossary below. These definitions are the essential terms that you must know and understand in order to prepare for an exam. The additional list of terms provides further definitions of

Guided tour of the companion website

 Book resources are available to download. Print your own **topic maps** and **revision checklists**!

 Use the **study plan** prior to your revision to help you assess how well you know the subject and determine which areas need most attention. Choose to take the full assessment or focus on targeted study units.

 'Test your knowledge' of individual areas with quizzes tailored specifically to each chapter. **Sample problem and essay questions** are also available with guidance on writing a good answer.

 Flashcards test and improve recall of important legal terms, key cases and statutes. Available in both electronic and printable formats.

'You be the marker' gives you the chance to evaluate sample exam answers for different question types and understand how and why an examiner awards marks.

Download the **podcast** and listen as your own personal Law Express tutor guides you through answering a typical but challenging question. A step-by-step explanation on how to approach the question is provided, including what essential elements your answer will need for a pass, how to structure a good response, and what to do to make your answer stand out so that you can earn extra marks.

All of this and more can be found when you visit
www.pearsoned.co.uk/lawexpress

Table of cases and statutes

◼ Cases

■ Statutes

Statutory instruments

European Union legislation

Listed in ascending date order

■ Conventions and Treaties

Copyright subsistence

1

Revision checklist

Essential points you should know:

- [ ] What amounts to originality
- [ ] What constitutes fixation
- [ ] What amounts to a copyright work
- [ ] What are secondary or derivative works
- [ ] The qualification requirements
- [ ] The duration of the copyright term

◼ Topic map

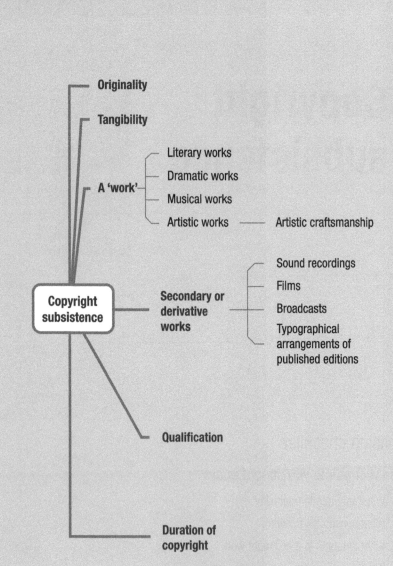

A printable version of this topic map is available from **www.pearsoned.co.uk/lawexpress**

■ Introduction

Copyright does not protect the idea but the independent expression of the idea.

Copyright does not create monopolies. It is intended to prevent others, for a defined period of time, from taking unfair advantage of a person's creative efforts. What will be protected is stipulated in the Copyright, Designs and Patents Act 1988. Although original literary works, films and sound recordings are all included, not all creative efforts are protected under the Act. This does mean that some highly original creations fall between the lines. The owner of the copyright has the exclusive right to do, or license others to do, certain acts in relation to the work. Apart from where certain exceptions exist, the owner or licensee may sue for infringement and obtain remedies such as an injunction and damages.

ASSESSMENT ADVICE

Essay questions

A possible essay question may ask you to discuss the difficulty in establishing a work as one of artistic craftsmanship. Keep in mind any other forms of intellectual property protection such as design right that could be available as an alternative to copyright protection. Another essay question could relate to the gap in protection for creative ideas seen in the *Norowzian* case and the split between the idea and the expression of a work.

Problem questions

A problem question could include a scenario where a work is put into tangible form by another, where there is a trivial or *de minimis* work or a work with no artistic merit. There may also be an issue raised relating to sound recordings including qualification and duration issues on both derivative and original works.

■ Sample question

Could you answer this question? Below is a typical essay question that could arise on this topic. Guidelines on answering the question are included at the end of this chapter, whilst a sample problem question and guidance on tackling it can be found on the companion website.

ESSAY QUESTION

The formats of television game shows and reality programmes, such as *Pop Idol* and *Big Brother*, are inadequately protected by copyright in the UK. The time is right to introduce format rights as a new type of copyright work.

Discuss with reference to decided cases.

■ Originality

Not all creative effort is protected. For protection the output must fall into the category of 'works' and must be **original**.

KEY STATUTE

Section 1 Copyright, Designs and Patents Act 1988

Copyright is a property right which subsists in original literary, dramatic, musical and artistic works as well as sound recordings, films, broadcasts and typographical arrangements of published editions.

KEY DEFINITION: Original

A work is original for copyright purposes if it has originated from the author and has not been copied from another work. For computer programs and copyright databases, a work is original if it is the author's own intellectual creation.

Originality for copyright purposes does not demand the novelty or innovation required in order to obtain a patent. For copyright, original means that the work originates from or is the intellectual creation of the **author**, its creator and it has not been copied from another's work. This is a low but minimum standard. A simplistic one-line drawing would be regarded as too trivial to merit copyright protection.

KEY CASE

Interlego AG v *Tyco Industries Inc.* **[1989] 1 AC 217, HL**

Concerning: whether small modifications made to existing drawings of 'Lego' bricks gave rise to a fresh copyright

Facts

The original Lego bricks had been patented and were registered as designs but these had expired. Some changes had been made to the design and these later bricks were copied by Tyco. Lego claimed copyright infringement.

Legal principle

For copyright to exist there must be an original work. Even though modifications are technically significant, if they are not visually significant and are in effect copies of existing works they would not give rise to a new copyright.

To hold otherwise would result in the possibility that copyright, in what was essentially the same work, could be extended indefinitely by merely making minor changes. Facts are not protected and a name such as Exxon cannot be subject to copyright even if a lot of work has gone into its creation. However, it has been held that headlines on an internet website arguably could be a literary work.

✎ EXAM TIP

Show an awareness of the practical consequences of copyright protection by pointing out that the failure to grant copyright for a single word is not just due to the *de minimis* principle. The intention in *Exxon* was to obtain greater protection over a range of goods or services via copyright than mere registration as a trade mark would have provided. There is also a public interest in preventing the control of words or phrases that should be available for all to use without fear of copyright infringement.

✓ Make your answer stand out

The *Infopaq* decision held that by taking 11 words, if those words were the result of the intellectual creation of the author, copyright infringement could occur. This view was reinforced in the *Meltwater* case on appeal. It has been argued that these decisions have changed the requirements for originality under the CDPA from 'sweat of the brow' to the 'intellectual creation of the author'. Make your answer stand out by explaining that it has been suggested that these cases have been misinterpreted and that although copying 11 words may infringe copyright, 11 words in themselves may not necessarily amount to a separate work of copyright (see Deming Liu (2013) and Rahmatian (2013)).

■ Tangibility

Copyright does not protect ideas, only a particular expression of an idea. Artistic works will usually be in tangible form, otherwise they could not be seen, but they do need some sort of surface to exist upon. In order to protect an idea in a literary, dramatic or musical work the expression must be recorded in a permanent form. This can be in writing or in any other way. All new methods of recording or fixation are covered in the Act.

KEY STATUTE

Section 3(2) and (3) Copyright, Designs and Patents Act 1988

Copyright does not subsist in a literary, dramatic or musical work unless and until it is recorded in writing or otherwise, that is, any other way. It is immaterial whether the work is recorded by or with the permission of the author.

There will be no copyright in an impromptu speech or a tune devised while playing the guitar unless they are recorded. The recording can be made by anyone, even without the permission of the author. On recording, fixation will take place and copyright will spring into existence.

□ REVISION NOTE

Who is the first owner of the copyright will be determined by who is the author of the work and their status. (Please refer to Chapter 2 on authorship and ownership.)

KEY CASE

Walter v *Lane* [1900] AC 539, HL

Concerning: the existence of copyright in an impromptu speech

Facts

The Earl of Rosebery made a speech. A reporter for *The Times* recorded it verbatim in shorthand, adding nothing apart from his reporting skills. The speech was published in *The Times* and copied by another. The issue was whether *The Times* had a right to sue for infringement.

Legal principle

The speaker was the author of the written work for copyright purposes. The reporter, having used skill and judgement in recording the speech using his own choice, sequence and combination of words, adding structure and punctuation, was the author of that report of the speech, an original work in its own right.

If the reporter had taped the speech on a tape machine he would have had copyright in the sound recording.

> **! Don't be tempted to . . .**
>
> Don't fail to understand that fixation can be made even without the knowledge or licence of the author of the 'work'. Make sure, however, that you do not confuse the situation of a secretary taking dictation, where they will not obtain copyright in the written work, and the reporter in *Walter* v *Lane*. Owing to the reporter expending extra skills in the reporting of the speech, copyright vested both in the author, the Earl, and the reporter. If the reporter had taken down only some ideas expressed in the speech there would have been no fixation of the expression of Lord Rosebery.

■ A 'work'

The Act is very specific about what can be protected.

Literary works

> **KEY STATUTE**
>
> **Section 3(1) Copyright, Designs and Patents Act 1988 (part)**
>
> A literary work is any work, other than a dramatic or musical work, which is written, spoken or sung, and includes a table or compilation (other than a database), a computer program, preparatory design material for a computer program and a database.

'Literary work' covers a work which is expressed in print or writing, irrespective of its quality. No merit is required. Selections, arrangements, raw research material and compilations of literary works are protected but only if they are recorded. There is no protection for compilations of drawings, as a literary work.

Dramatic works

> **KEY STATUTE**
>
> **Section 3(1) Copyright, Designs and Patents Act 1988 (part)**
>
> 'A "dramatic" work includes a work of dance or mime.'

The dialogue of a dramatic work on its own is protected by literary copyright. A work of mime without words can be protected as a dramatic work. But there can be problems with outputs that do not fit the criteria of 'work'.

KEY CASE

Norowzian v *Arks Ltd* **[2000] FSR 363, CA**

Concerning: what constitutes a dramatic work

Facts

Mr Norowzian made the film *Joy*. It showed a man dancing and used 'flash framing' and 'jump cutting' (removing bits of film). Due to these editing techniques the dancing looked surreal. The man was doing things that in real time he could not have performed before an audience, hence this was not a dramatic work and was incapable of copyright protection.

Legal principle

The content of the film can be a dramatic work if it is 'a work of action with or without words or music which is capable of being performed before an audience'. A film itself can be a work of action and be performed before an audience.

A film is a dramatic work distinct from the script. Rhythm, pace and movement are ideas, and cannot be protected as only the specific expression of the idea is covered. A similar problem of 'slipping through the net' is found in television game-show formats. Often these comprise stock phrases or events which are interjected at appropriate times. For copyright to arise there must be fixation, a script recorded in permanent form. This is not appropriate to game-shows, which are expected to be spontaneous.

❗ Don't be tempted to . . .

Don't assume that all creative effort is protected by copyright. If the purpose of copyright is to protect creative effort, it is not doing so. By being so prescriptive in what is a 'work', UK copyright law may fail to provide protection for all creativity. This is of particular note in the fashion industry.

Musical works

For copyright purposes music and lyrics are separate. Lyrics are protected as literary works, so what is left is the music. The copyright can be owned by different people and expire at different times.

KEY STATUTE

Section 3(1) Copyright, Designs and Patents Act 1988 (part)

'A musical work is one consisting of music, exclusive of any words or action intended to be sung, spoken or performed with the music.'

There is, as with most of the other 'original' works, no quality requirement, and even a few notes may attract copyright. They must, however, be original. They may still be regarded as original musical works even if they are based on an existing piece of music. Such adaptations or transcriptions will attract their own copyright if the minimum amount of skill and labour has gone into their creation. It may be found, however, that the adaptation or transcription infringes the copyright in the earlier musical work if made without the permission of the owner.

KEY CASE

Hyperion Records Ltd v *Sawkins* [2005] RPC 32, CA

Concerning: whether a new copyright had been created by substantial editing

Facts

Dr Sawkins wrote new performing editions of some musical compositions that had gone out of copyright. He added some new aspects and changed some notes to make them possible to play. His intention was to recreate the music as originally written, as a complete and accurate score of the music did not exist. Hyperion re-recorded the music without the permission of Dr Sawkins, claiming that there was no copyright as it had expired. They were found to have infringed Dr Sawkins's copyright.

Legal principle

Looking at the work as a whole this was not merely transcription. The notes are not the only expression that is protected by copyright. Other elements contribute to the sound of the music when performed and they can be protected if they are the product of an author's effort, skill and time.

 Make your answer stand out

The distinction between interpretation and composition, and the relationship between the cases of *Interlego* and *Sawkins* is a difficult one to make. For a clear summary of the problems associated with originality and when a separate copyright will arise when there has been restoration or reconstruction see Torremans (2011).

Artistic works

Copyright subsists in an artistic work irrespective of artistic quality. It will cover purely utilitarian or functional works as well as 'works of art'. This is not the case with works of artistic craftsmanship, where more than originality and fixation is needed for copyright to arise.

KEY STATUTE

Section 4(1) and (2) Copyright, Designs and Patents Act 1988

An artistic work means a graphic work (painting, drawing, diagram, map, chart or plan), a photograph, sculpture (which includes a cast or model made for the purposes of sculpture), collage, all irrespective of artistic quality. It also includes a work of architecture (a building; a fixed structure or a model for a building) or a work of artistic craftsmanship.

We can see that the meaning of 'sculpture' is very wide but it must be a three-dimensional work and some regard has to be had to the normal use of the word. The wooden models used as a mould to make the Frisbee were held to be sculptures but the Supreme Court (*Lucasfilm Ltd* v *Ainsworth*, the *Star Wars* case) confirmed that this and some other cases on sculptures were wrongly decided. An artist must be involved in the creation of a sculpture. There must be an underlying intention that the three-dimensional object should have some visual appeal but, remember, it need not have artistic worth. Being functional in addition to having visual appeal will not prevent an object from being a sculpture. Purely functional items such as the helmets worn by the Imperial Stormtroopers in the *Star Wars* films were held not to be sculptures but could have been protected under unregistered design law.

Artistic craftsmanship

Many items could be regarded as works of craftsmanship, such as jewellery or hand-knitted jumpers. By including the word 'artistic' in section 4(1) some artistic quality is obviously required in order to gain copyright protection.

! **Don't be tempted to . . .**

Don't forget that artistic works, especially works of artistic craftsmanship, present a category that causes special problems because it overlaps with design law. Make sure that you make it clear that the relationship between copyright and design law is *not at all* clear-cut.

> **KEY CASE**
>
> *George Hensher Ltd* v *Restawhile Upholstery Ltd* [1974] AC 64, HL
> *Concerning: what is needed to be a work of artistic craftsmanship*
>
> **Facts**
>
> The claimant made a rough prototype for a suite of furniture in order to show how it was going to look when produced. The defendant copied the prototype and was unsuccessfully sued for copyright infringement as the work did not fit into the category of artistic craftsmanship.
>
> **Legal principle**
>
> There was no one legal principle to determine artistic craftsmanship, but solutions offered by the court were:
>
> 1. It must give pleasure and be valued for its appearance.
> 2. It is up to the court to decide after talking to expert witnesses.
> 3. The author must be consciously trying to create a work of art.
> 4. There must be genuine craftsmanship involved.

It seems that the designer must be trying to make the product have some artistic or at least aesthetic appeal. Alternatively, it must give pleasure to others, possibly due to its skilled craftsmanship. Such an intention of course could not have existed when making a rough mock-up. We are left with a considerable amount of uncertainty in this area.

> 📖 **REVISION NOTE**
>
> Even though many of these more industrial works will fail to be classed as works of artistic craftsmanship, they may be protected either as Community designs, the UK registered design or under the UK unregistered design right. (See Chapter 7.)

■ Secondary or derivative works

Sound recordings, films and broadcasts

Derivative works are usually, but do not have to be, based on original works which may have their own separate copyright. Derivative works typically protect the entrepreneur rather than the author of a work. It is the entrepreneur who will take any infringement proceedings if the work is copied. There is no requirement that these works are original but sound recordings and films are required to be recordings, broadly defined.

Sound recordings

> **KEY STATUTE**
>
> **Section 5A Copyright, Designs and Patents Act 1988**
>
> (1)(a) 'Sound recordings must be a recording of sounds from which sounds may be reproduced'.

A sound recording of, for example, birdsong, though not a 'work' as defined under the Act, would also gain protection. There is no quality requirement.

Films

> **KEY STATUTE**
>
> **Section 5B Copyright, Designs and Patents Act 1988**
>
> Film means 'a recording on any medium from which a moving image may be produced'. The soundtrack accompanying a film is part of the film.

As well as the film on a 'medium', such as videotape or celluloid, being protected, a film is also protected as a dramatic work (*Norowzian* v *Arks*). The soundtrack of a film is regarded as part of the film. There is, however, copyright only in the master copy of the film or sound recording. This prevents a potential everlasting copyright which would otherwise result if a new copyright arose every time a CD or videotape is reproduced.

Broadcasts

> **KEY STATUTE**
>
> **Section 6 Copyright, Designs and Patents Act 1988**
>
> Broadcast means an electronic transmission of visual images, sound or other information which is transmitted either for simultaneous reception by members of the public and capable of being lawfully received by them, or transmitted at a time determined solely by the person making the transmission for presentation to members of the public.

Most forms of internet transmission, where the person receiving the transmission does so at a place and at a time chosen by that person, are not regarded as broadcasts, being excluded by section 6(1A). However, conventional radio or television broadcasts are included. No fixation is required. Satellite broadcasts by their very nature can reach other countries. They may there be rebroadcast to further countries before being finally broadcast to the public. They are regarded as broadcasts even if they are encrypted, as long as the public has had the decoding equipment lawfully made available to them. The law governing the broadcast is to be that of the country from where the original broadcast was made, where the uplink station is situated.

Typographical arrangements of published editions

A book may be of an original work but the typographical arrangement, the layout, font and lettering of the page, will attract its own separate copyright. This copyright will exist even if the original work is out of copyright unless it is a mere copy of a previous text. The whole book, dramatic or musical work is protected. This means the entire 'between the covers' work. So taking an article from a newspaper is not an infringement of the typographical arrangement as it is not sufficiently substantial.

■ Qualification

Works have to pass one more hurdle in order to gain copyright protection in the UK. Not only must the work be original and in tangible form but it must also be a qualifying work. Due to the Berne Convention, the Universal Copyright Convention and the Trade-related Aspects of Intellectual Property Rights (TRIPs) agreement authors connected with another Member State are to be treated in the same way as a Member State's own authors and should receive the same copyright. Either the author of the work, or the country of first publication (so the work must actually be published), or, in the case of a broadcast, the country of first transmission must have some connection with a Member State.

KEY STATUTE

Sections 154 and 155 Copyright, Designs and Patents Act 1988

A work will qualify for copyright protection either if the author is a British citizen, domiciled or resident in the UK or a body incorporated under the law of the UK or a qualifying country or if the work was first published or published simultaneously in a qualifying country.

Either the author has a connection with a qualifying country or the work was first published in a qualifying country. Even if the work is first published in a non-qualifying country it will be regarded as first published for qualification purposes if it was then published in a qualifying country within 30 days of that initial publication. To amount to publication, sufficient copies must be issued to the public to satisfy reasonable demands. So if the public shows little demand for the work, few copies need be made available to qualify for publication status.

■ Duration of copyright

The duration of copyright in most of the 'original works' and in films is life of the author plus 70 years, at least 70 years for sound recordings, 50 years for broadcasts and 25 years for typographical arrangements of published editions. The duration of copyright in certain types of artistic works that have been commercially exploited is also 25 years. The term expires at the end of the relevant calendar year.

■ Putting it all together

Answer guidelines

See the essay question at the start of the chapter.

Approaching the question

This is a reform type question. This means that you must talk about what the law is and any weaknesses that exist in it at the present.

Important points to include

- Some of the further reading on page 15 would be helpful in answering this question.
- The key case which indicated that television show formats were not adequately protected by copyright was the Privy Council decision in *Green* v *Broadcasting Corp. of New Zealand*, the *Opportunity Knocks* case. This is a useful starting point for the discussion.
- Identify in that case why the format was not protected. For example, written scripts had not been produced in evidence and the format as claimed was described as being too uncertain.
- Consider and discuss other cases such as *Norowzian* v *Arks*, the 'jump-cutting' film.
- Note that lack of protection means that countries such as the USA, Australia and New Zealand can copy formats of UK television shows. For example, New Zealand makes *Popstars* which is very similar to *Pop Idol*.
- It would be useful to consider cases on non-literal copying, such as *Nova Productions Ltd* v *Mazooma Games Ltd* and *IPC Media Ltd* v *Highbury Leisure Publishing (No. 2)*, where what was being claimed in reality was that the format of the video game and glossy magazine had been copied.

✓ Make your answer stand out

Consider what, if anything, producers of television shows could do to acquire some protection through copyright law.

Set out your views on whether copyright should be extended to include formats as a distinct type of copyright and the implications this might have, for example, by making it difficult to bring out rival 'copycat' shows. Point out the difficulty of establishing causality in this type of industry.

READ TO IMPRESS

Clark, S. (2009) '*Lucasfilm Ltd and Others* v *Ainsworth and Another*: the force of copyright protection for three-dimensional designs as sculptures or works of artistic craftsmanship', 31(7) *EIPR*, 384.

Fields, D. (2011) 'Come and have a go . . . if you think you are smart enough', 22(2) *Entertainment Law Review*, 61.

Gravells, N. (2007) 'Authorship and originality: the persistent influence of *Walter* v *Lane*', 3 *Intellectual Property Quarterly*, 267.

Harding, I. (2013) 'Fashion and copyright: weaving our way towards increased protection' 35(4) *EIPR*, 183.

Klement, U. (2007) 'Protecting television show formats under copyright law – new developments in common law and civil law countries', 29(2) *EIPR*, 52.

Liu, D. (2013) 'Meltwater melts not water but principle!' 35(6) *EIPR*, 327.

Rahmatian, A. (2013) 'Originality in UK Copyright Law: The Old "Skill and Labour" Doctrine Under Pressure' 44(1) *IIC*, 4.

Steffensen, T. (2000) 'Rights to TV formats – from a copyright and marketing law perspective', 11(5) *Entertainment Law Review*, 85.

Torremans, P. (2011) 'Legal issues pertaining to the restoration and reconstitution of manuscripts, sheet music, paintings and films for marketing purposes' 33(3) *EIPR*, 178.

www.pearsoned.co.uk/lawexpress
Go online to access more revision support including quizzes to test your knowledge, sample questions with answer guidelines, podcasts you can download, and more!

Authorship, ownership and moral rights

2

Revision checklist

Essential points you should know:

- [ ] Authorship and joint authorship
- [ ] Author or employer as first owner
- [ ] Beneficial ownership and implied licences
- [ ] The paternity right
- [ ] The integrity right
- [ ] False attribution of a work
- [ ] Right to privacy in photographs and films
- [ ] Artists' resale right

■ Topic map

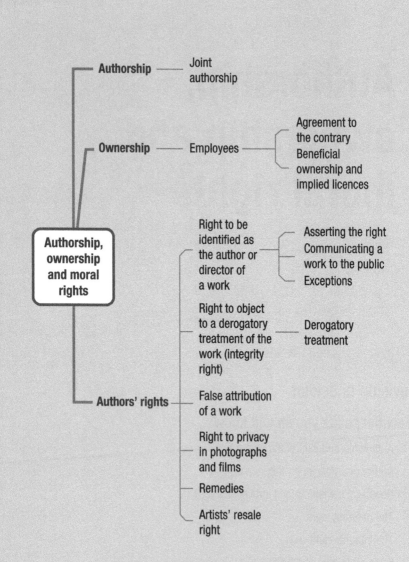

■ Introduction

The identity of an author will determine first ownership and consequently the duration of both the copyright and moral rights in the work.

In order to exploit copyright you must have the right to do so by ownership or licence. The author, the person who creates the work, is normally the first owner of the copyright. However, if the work was created in the course of employment, the employer will usually be the first owner of the copyright. Two independent rights exist: moral rights, which may be retained by the author even though ownership has been assigned, and an economic right, the right to exploit the work. The owner or author may exploit the work himself or may grant a licence (retaining ownership), or assign (transferring ownership), the copyright to another.

ASSESSMENT ADVICE

Essay questions

An essay question may well ask you to consider the weakness of the moral rights that have been given to authors in the UK. The vulnerable bargaining position of the author and the fact that many of these rights can be waived is of significance. You must keep in mind when answering such a question that very strong rights for authors reduce the efficiency with which the entrepreneur can exploit the work that has been assigned to him. Strengthening the moral rights may have an impact on the willingness of the entrepreneur to commercialise the author's work in the long term.

Problem questions

Many copyright works are created by employees during the course of their employment. It is highly likely that there will be some issue relating to the rights of first ownership in any problem question set in this area. Problems around unintentional joint authorship may also be included and you must be able to establish clearly the elements that are needed to be regarded as a joint author rather than a mere provider of ideas.

◼ Sample question

Could you answer this question? Below is a typical problem question that could arise on this topic. Guidelines on answering the question are included at the end of this chapter, whilst a sample essay question and guidance on tackling it can be found on the companion website.

PROBLEM QUESTION

Adrian wrote the music and lyrics for a song called 'Bad'. Having trouble with the drum beat he heard Betty, a carpenter, hammering in the house next door. Inviting Betty into his studio he asked her to hammer while he played the tune in time to her rhythm. He recorded the resulting music. Adrian sold the song to BMI but is upset that they have made his 'Grime' music into a ballad. He feels that his reputation as a 'Grime' musician has been destroyed. Adrian has discovered that Chris has produced a CD in which Adrian is falsely said to be the author of the song 'Nasty'. Betty has seen that one of her wedding photographs taken by Happy Day Photos is featured on the cover of Chris's CD.

Discuss.

◼ Authorship

The author of an original work is the person who created it. The author of a compilation is the person who gathers or organises the material contained within the compilation, while each separate contribution will have its own separate author.

KEY STATUTE

Section 9(1) Copyright, Designs and Patents Act 1988

The author is the person who created the work. For a sound recording the author is taken to be the producer, for a film it is the producer and principal director, for a broadcast it is the person making it, for a typographical arrangement it is the publisher. For a computer-generated literary, dramatic, musical or artistic work it is the person who made the arrangements necessary for its creation. A work will be held to be of unknown authorship if it is not possible to identify the author (or any of them in the case of a work of joint authorship) after making reasonable enquiries.

The author is the person who puts in the right sort of effort, skill and labour into the creation or expression of the work. There must be that essential creative input, a 'direct responsibility for what actually appears on the paper'. An amanuensis or secretary taking dictation, although responsible for fixation, is not the author of the work.

📖 REVISION NOTE

Please refer to Chapter 1 for some discussion on fixation and the case of *Walter* v *Lane*.

Joint authorship

If two or more people have collaborated to create a work so that it is impossible to identify each author's contribution, this will result in a work of **joint authorship**.

KEY STATUTE

Section 10(1) Copyright, Designs and Patents Act 1988

A work is of joint authorship if produced by the collaboration of two or more authors and the contribution of each is not distinct from that of the others.

The authors need not have intended to create a work of joint authorship and their contributions need not be equal. But they must have intended to create a work.

KEY CASE

Fisher v *Brooker* [2009] FSR 25, HL
Concerning: a claim to joint authorship

Facts

Mr Fisher wrote the distinctive organ part in the famous song 'Whiter Shade of Pale' recorded by Procul Harum. The part had originally been written for piano but had been considerably reworked by Mr Fisher. Over 30 years later, Mr Fisher claimed joint authorship of the song.

Legal principle

Joint authorship may result from reworking an existing work by a person if his input can be regarded as an original contribution to the work. Mr Fisher was entitled to 40% share in the copyright but could not claim back-royalties because his silence prior to making his claim gave rise to a gratuitous licence.

✎ EXAM TIP

Show that you understand the practical significance of this decision. This case demonstrates how important it is to make sure that copyright authorship and ownership is clarified where several persons have contributed to the creation or modification of a work. In some cases, it may be appropriate to execute a formal assignment of copyright.

To be a joint author each must have made a significant contribution in terms of the right sort of creative skill and judgement. Merely editing, contributing suggestions, ideas and information will not give rise to a finding of joint authorship.

KEY CASE

Robin Ray v *Classic FM plc* **[1998] FSR 622 ChD**

Concerning: the type of contribution needed to become a joint author

Facts

Robin Ray was an expert on classical music and, after discussion of what was needed, created a playlist of music for the use of the radio station Classic FM. Classic FM failed in their claim that they were joint authors of the list, having provided the ideas. Copyright does not exist in ideas but the expression of the ideas, and Ray had not only written down but was also solely responsible for the ideas found in the playlist.

Legal principle

To be a joint author there must be a significant creative contribution which was incorporated into the finished work. 'Although penmanship did not have to be exercised, a joint author had to have direct responsibility for what ended up on the paper which was the equivalent to penmanship' (Lightman J).

This case is also important in setting out guidelines to be applied to determine whether a beneficial assignment or implied licence is appropriate.

Each of the joint authors will have their own copyright in the work, which, if an original work, will last for the life of the longest to live plus 70 years. Although a joint author can leave their share on death, consent of all the **co-authors** must be obtained in order to license the work.

KEY DEFINITION: Joint/co-authorship

A work of joint authorship is where the contribution of each author cannot be separated, whereas the contribution of each author in a work of co-authorship is distinct, discrete and separately distinguishable.

■ Ownership

Subject to some exceptions, the author of a work is the first owner of the copyright.

> **KEY STATUTE**
>
> **Section 11(1) and (2) Copyright, Designs and Patents Act 1988**
>
> The author of a work is the first owner of any copyright in it. However, if made by an employee in the course of their employment, the employer is the first owner of any copyright subject to any agreement to the contrary. Note other rules apply in relation to Crown Copyright, Parliamentary Copyright and copyright of certain international organisations, such as the United Nations.

The main difficulty with the ownership provisions concerns the employer/employee relationship and the meaning of 'in the course of his employment'.

Employees

The job description in the contract of employment is important. A person employed in a factory who writes poetry in their spare time is not employed as a poet and the poems are not written in the course of their employment. They, not their employer, will be the first owner of the copyright in the poems. However, if the employee is employed under a contract with a very wide job description as a researcher, copyright in a research proposal will probably belong to the employer, even if the employee created the work on his own initiative outside normal working hours.

> **KEY CASE**
>
> *Stephenson Jordan & Harrison Ltd* v *MacDonald* [1952] RPC 10, CA
> *Concerning: whether copyright belonged to an employee or employer*
>
> **Facts**
>
> An accountant started to give lectures. He published them in a book. Although his employer had provided secretarial help when he was writing the book, he nevertheless owned the copyright in the book. He was employed to advise clients. Giving lectures was not part of his normal duties and he had not been instructed by his employers either to give the lectures or produce the book. The copyright in a report written for a client as part of the employee's duties and incorporated into a part of the book did, however, belong to the employer.
>
> **Legal principle**
>
> Merely using the facilities of an employer does not entitle the employer to copyright in an employee's creation if it was not made in the course of their duties as an employee.

You should ask whether the skill, effort and judgement expended by the employee in creating the work are part of the employee's normal duties (express or implied) or within any special duties assigned to him by the employer. If they are not, the employee will be the first owner of the copyright, even if he has used his employer's facilities when creating the work.

Agreement to the contrary

If there is an agreement to the contrary, either express or implied, the employee may remain the first owner of the copyright.

> **✎ EXAM TIP**
>
> Normally in a transfer of ownership an assignment will not be effective unless it is in writing and signed by the previous owner. However, no writing is needed where an employer as first owner agrees to the employee who created the work being the first owner, for example, in the case of an implied agreement to this effect.

The agreement to the contrary would usually be between the employer and the employee but if the employee has done work on behalf of a third party it may be between the employer and the third party. If the employee's name appears on the work, or copies of the work, there is a presumption that the work was not made in the course of employment.

Beneficial ownership and implied licences

If a consultant has been commissioned to create a work, they are *not* an employee and the commissioner, unlike an employer, has no automatic right to the copyright in the work. The commissioner may not realise that to obtain copyright in the work a written **assignment** would need to have been made. In some circumstances the court may decide that it is equitable to hold that the commissioner is entitled to **beneficial ownership** of the copyright or that a licence should be implied.

> **✎ EXAM TIP**
>
> Issues of ownership of copyright are common in exam questions. Make sure you know the rules under the statute and can apply them to practical situations. Also ensure you are familiar with case law on ownership. This is an area where students often fall down.

Blair v *Osborne & Tomkins* [1971] 1 All ER 468, CA

Concerning: an implied licence to use a commissioned work

Facts

The owner of land commissioned architects to make plans in order to obtain planning permission to build houses. The owners then sold the land. The purchasers asked surveyors to modify the plans and then used them to build the houses.

Legal principle

Although architects normally retain the copyright in their plans, there may be an implied licence so as to permit the use of the work for its intended purpose.

! Don't be tempted to . . .

Don't think that beneficial assignments of copyright are always appropriate where a person (not being the creator's employer) has commissioned the creation of a work of copyright. A basic principle is that the courts will only grant the minimum necessary to give effect to the presumed intention of the parties. In many cases, justice will be satisfied by the grant of a limited implied licence allowing the continued use of the work in question by the person commissioning its creation.

■ Authors' rights

UK copyright law has traditionally emphasised the economic rights associated with copyright. Efficient exploitation of the work requires as much freedom for the entrepreneur as possible. However, this emphasis on the rights of the entrepreneur created an imbalance and this has been in part rectified by the introduction of the moral rights. They give authors some stake in their work after they have assigned ownership and no longer have control over how it is used. These moral rights are the right to be acknowledged as the author, the right to object to modification and derogatory treatment of the work, a right not to have another's work falsely attributed to them and a right to privacy in certain photographs and films.

Although on the face of it these rights seem to be of great benefit to the authors of works, they lose much of their force as they can be waived. Many authors are not capable of exploiting their own works and must assign them. They may be under great pressure from the entrepreneur to waive these moral rights to allow unfettered use of the work. Some rights may fail for lack of positive assertion on the part of the author or director. There is in addition the *droit de suite* (**artists' resale right**), which gives authors of works of art and manuscripts a **royalty** when the work is resold.

Right to be identified as the author or director of a work

Sometimes referred to as the 'paternity right', this is the right of the person who brought the work to life.

KEY STATUTE

Sections 77–79 Copyright, Designs and Patents Act 1988

The author of an original work or the director of a film has the right to be identified as the author or director of the work. The right arises when the work or an adaptation of the work is published commercially, performed in public, or copies of a film, sound recording or graphic work representing a work of architecture are issued to or communicated to the public.

The right must be asserted either at the time of the assignment or licensing of the copyright or in writing signed by the author.

There are exceptions to the right which include computer programs, computer-generated works, works created during the course of employment where the act in question was done with the authorisation of the copyright owner, in respect of the fair dealing exceptions or where it would be impractical to include the author's name with the publication.

Asserting the right

The right to be identified as the author of an 'original' work or as the director of a film does not arise automatically; it must be asserted. The right applies in relation to the whole or any substantial part of the work which is in copyright. 'Substantial' in the context of moral rights will have the same meaning as applies for economic rights.

📖 REVISION NOTE

See Chapter 3 for a discussion on the meaning of 'substantial'.

The identification must be clear and reasonably prominent. An artist putting their name or a pseudonym on a painting is asserting their right. Although the paternity right may be asserted at any time during the life of the author, this assertion will only bind those with notice of it if made after assignment.

Hyperion Records Ltd v *Dr Lionel Sawkins* [2005] RPC 32, CA

Concerning: form of acknowledgement specified by author (or film director)

Facts

Dr Sawkins had expressly specified the acknowledgement '© Copyright 2002 by Lionel Sawkins' to be used on copies of CDs of performing editions of ancient music arranged by him. The publisher used the phrase 'With thanks to Dr Lionel Sawkins for his preparation of performance materials for this recording'.

Legal principle

Where a specific form of acknowledgement is required by the author (or director), failure to use this form will infringe the author's right to be identified as such.

Once asserted, the right to be identified as the author springs into action. However, the right only relates to the commercialisation of the work and does not apply to derivative works.

Communicating a work to the public

Communicating a work to the public means communication to the public by any means, including broadcasting. Non-commercial exploitation, such as the private performance of a play, does not give rise to the obligation to identify the author. But once asserted, *every* commercial publication must be accompanied by the name of the author of the initial work.

Exceptions

There is a long list of exceptions to the right to be identified. They include computer programs, computer-generated works, newspapers, encyclopaedias and an exception relating to works created by employees in the course of their employment in relation to acts authorised. It is felt that without these exceptions the exploitation of the work could be hampered by so many people asserting their moral rights. There are also fair dealing exceptions where the right to be identified as the author will not be enforced.

Right to object to derogatory treatment of the work (integrity right)

Sections 80–83 Copyright, Designs and Patents Act 1988

The author of an original work and a director of a film have the right not to have their work subjected to derogatory treatment. Treatment means the addition to, deletion from, alteration to or adaptation of the work but does not include translation, arrangement ▶

or transcription which is merely a change of key or register of a musical work. Treatment is derogatory if it amounts to distortion or mutilation of the work or is prejudicial to the honour or reputation of the author or director.

The right only applies if the derogatory treatment of the original work is published commercially or is issued to the public.

There are exceptions for computer-related works and works created for the purpose of reporting current events, where it would be impractical to apply the right.

The right only applies if the author has been identified and if no disclaimer has been included.

The 'integrity right' applies to works that are in copyright and benefits the same people as the paternity right but need not be asserted.

Derogatory treatment

Writing a new edition of a book can be regarded as 'treatment'. Derogatory treatment is a treatment which amounts to distortion or mutilation of the work. The work itself must be altered. It is not enough that the work is displayed in a way that would be regarded as derogatory. However, distortion or mutilation of the work itself is not enough. There must also be prejudice to the honour or reputation of the author.

KEY CASE

Confetti Records v *Warner Music UK Ltd* **[2003] EMLR 35, CA**
Concerning: derogatory treatment

Facts

A rap version of the song 'Burnin', was made by the group Heartless Crew. The rap version contained references to violence and drugs which the court found very difficult to decipher. The original composer Mr Alcee unsuccessfully claimed that the addition of the rap lyrics was a derogatory treatment of his work.

Legal principle

There must be some damage to the author's honour or reputation.

'I hold that the mere fact that a work has been distorted or mutilated gives rise to no claim, unless the distortion or mutilation prejudices the author's honour or reputation' (Mr Justice Lewison).

It is not up to the author but to right-thinking members of the public to decide whether the reputation of the author has been prejudiced by the derogatory treatment. As with the paternity right there are exceptions, and the right does not apply to computer programs and computer-generated works or in relation to any work made for the purpose of reporting current events, newspapers, magazines, encyclopaedias, or to employees. It is felt that being able to object to such treatment in these areas would cause potential delay in publishing these works.

False attribution of a work

This right is again concerned with commercial not private communications.

KEY STATUTE

Section 84 Copyright, Designs and Patents Act 1988

The author of an original work and directors of a film have the right not to have a work either expressly or impliedly falsely attributed to them. The right applies if the falsely attributed work is issued to the public by a person who knows or has reason to believe that the attribution is false.

The right also applies if in the course of a business a person knowingly possesses or deals with the work or a copy of the work which contains the false attribution.

The false attribution right applies to original works and films, as do the other moral rights. There are no exceptions so it is also relevant to computer programs and typefaces. Although the claimant does not need to be mentioned by name, it can be used where B writes a book and pretends it, or parts of it, were written by A. False attribution does not relate to a work created by the person asserting it. As A, the person falsely attributed, has no copyright in the work its duration is not the life of the author plus 70 years but only 20 years after the death of A, the person to whom the work is attributed falsely. There is also a right of action against anyone who possesses or deals with a copy of the work in the course of business if they know or have reason to believe that there is a false attribution.

Right to privacy in photographs and films

There is no general right to privacy in English law. When someone commissions a photograph it is the photographer who is the first owner of the copyright in the photograph. The photographer has control over the negatives and can use them for his or her own purposes even against the wishes of the commissioner unless the photograph is taken or the film is made for private and domestic purposes.

KEY STATUTE

Section 85 Copyright, Designs and Patents Act 1988

A person who commissions the taking of a photograph or the making of a film for private and domestic purpose has the right not to have copies of the work issued, exhibited, shown or communicated to the public.

The right to privacy applies in the case of a photograph or film which is in copyright. The photograph must have been taken only for private and domestic purposes. It must have been commissioned. The right will not apply if a photographer took a photograph entirely on his own initiative or the subject of the photograph was included incidentally. The photographer does not need to be a professional photographer and the term is for the work itself, life of the author, the photographer, plus 70 years.

> **✎ EXAM TIP**
>
> To demonstrate a greater understanding of the interrelationship of different intellectual property rights, you could point out that the claimants in the case of *Douglas* v *Hello!* could not use this right. The photographs of the celebrity wedding had been intended to be sold commercially.

Remedies

Injunctions and damages are normally available for a breach of a statutory duty. If there has been an infringement of moral rights, damages would be for non-economic loss because moral rights are not economic in nature. An appropriate remedy may be to require a disclaimer dissociating the author or director from any derogatory treatment of their work.

Artists' resale right

This right was brought in under the Artists Resale Right Regulations 2006/346 implementing an EU Directive. It applies to original works of graphic or *plastic* art such as paintings and sculptures that are still in copyright. It does not apply if the work is sold privately. The author is given a right which they may not transfer or waive but may be transmitted on death. The author of the work is entitled to receive a royalty payable by the seller which is a percentage of the resale price, up to a maximum which is at present €12,500.

Licensing of orphan works

An orphan work is one where the copyright owner (or any of the owners in the case of a jointly owned work) cannot be found after a diligent search. The Enterprise and Regulatory Reform Act 2013 inserted new sections in the Copyright, Designs and Patents Act 1988 to deal with orphan works in compliance with the Directive on certain permitted uses of orphan works. Anyone wanting to make use of an orphan work will have to apply to an authorising body for a non-exclusive licence and pay a licence fee. The fine detail requires secondary legislation.

■ Putting it all together

Answer guidelines

See the problem question at the start of the chapter.

Approaching the question

Identify that this problem question concerns ownership of copyright in the original works and moral rights of authors of original works.

Before ownership of copyright can be determined, students must first apply the rules as to authorship and joint authorship. Notice that moral rights of 'paternity' and 'integrity' are engaged in respect of the music.

As is often the case in problem questions, there are gaps in the facts. Here, we are not told enough to work out who is entitled to the copyright in the photograph, but there may be extra points for dealing with it – for example, that the photographer would be the first owner (unless an employee creating it in the course of his or her employment) though Betty may now own it through an assignment and, if so, can bring an action for copyright infringement.

In context, however, it is clear that the issue of privacy in photographs taken for private and domestic purposes is relevant and must be addressed. Do not forget that Betty has the right of privacy only if she commissioned the taking of the photograph. If she did not commission the photograph, whoever did has the right (for example, if it was the groom or her father).

Important points to include

■ Adrian is the author and therefore first owner of the copyright in the song 'Bad' (s. 9).

■ If it is impossible to identify each author's contribution (s. 10) and Betty had contributed the right sort of skill and labour and intellectual creativity into creating the beat and if the intention had been to create a 'work', she could be a joint owner of the song (*Fisher* v *Brooker*). Merely contributing ideas would not be sufficient; she must be responsible for what was actually recorded (*Ray* v *Classic FM*).

■ Adrian could claim that his integrity right will be infringed if the altered work is issued to the public (ss. 80–83). He must prove that there has been some derogatory treatment to the work itself. It is not up to him but up to the right-thinking member of the public to feel that his honour or reputation has been prejudiced by the derogatory treatment (*Confetti Records*). Here it is unlikely ▶

that such a person would feel that such alteration would be sufficiently derogatory to his reputation.

- Adrian can also complain that Chris has made a false attribution by falsely claiming he is the author of 'Nasty'. This right will last for 20 years after Adrian's death.

- Betty has a right to privacy in her wedding photos as long as she commissioned Happy Day Photos to take them and they were intended purely for domestic purposes, unlike *Douglas* v *Hello!*

✓ Make your answer stand out

- Point out that Adrian should have asked Betty to assign her rights to him.

- Also mention that Chris's record company will be dealing with copies and so they can also be sued.

- Explain that although Betty may be able to take advantage of the privacy right if there had been an intention to use the photographs commercially, as in *Douglas* v *Hello!*, this right would not be available.

READ TO IMPRESS

Calleja, R. (2005) 'Copyright: equitable owners of copyright in Dr Martens–AirWair logo', 16(5) *Entertainment Law Review*, N44.

Chan, P. (2007) 'Moral rights in university students' academic works', 2(3) *Journal of Intellectual Property Law and Practice*, 174.

Longdin, L. (2005) 'Collaborative authorship of distance learning materials: cross-border copyright and moral rights problems', 27(1) *EIPR*, 4.

Roggero, C. (2011) 'Colourisation and the right to preserve the integrity of a film: a comparative study between civil and common law' 22(1) *Entertainment Law Review*, 25.

www.pearsoned.co.uk/lawexpress

Go online to access more revision support including quizzes to test your knowledge, sample questions with answer guidelines, podcasts you can download, and more!

Copyright infringement, remedies and defences

3

Revision checklist

Essential points you should know:

- [ ] The acts restricted by copyright
- [ ] What amounts to copying and the communication of a work to the public
- [ ] Secondary infringements of copyright
- [ ] Remedies for infringement of copyright
- [ ] Assessment of damages
- [ ] Injunctions against service providers having actual knowledge of infringement
- [ ] The Digital Economy Act 2010 and persistent online infringers
- [ ] Defences to copyright infringement and the permitted acts

■ Topic map

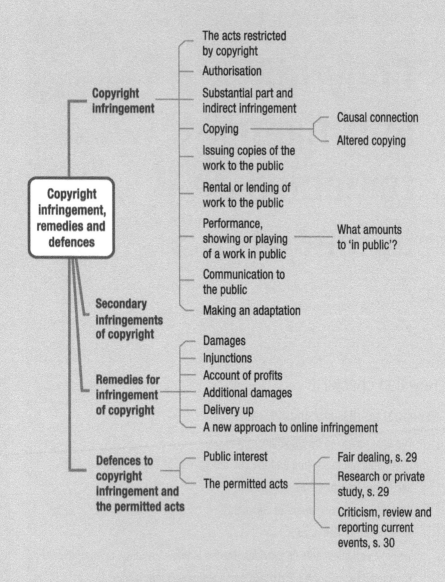

■ Introduction

Copyright infringement is performing (or authorising) any of the restricted acts to the whole or a substantial part of the work without the owner's licence in the absence of a defence or relevant permitted act.

The owner of copyright is given exclusive rights in respect of certain specified restricted acts. If any of these acts are done to the whole or a substantial part of the work without the licence of the owner, there will be a primary infringement of the copyright. There are other activities, mainly of a commercial nature, such as dealing with infringing copies of a work. These are described as secondary infringements. It is also an infringement if you authorise another to do a restricted act. There are not only civil remedies but also, in some cases, criminal penalties. The criminal offences generally, though not exactly, mirror the secondary infringements of copyright. There are some defences to copyright infringement and numerous exceptions to infringement known as the permitted acts.

ASSESSMENT ADVICE

Essay questions

You may be asked to discuss the difficulty in establishing what is a substantial amount of a work for infringement purposes. Alternatively, the balance between protecting the author of a work and the need for freedom of expression in relation to the fair dealing defences may also be a possible question.

Problem questions

This is a prime area for problem questions. A scenario where there has been some conscious or unconscious infringement, possibly an adaptation or, alternatively, altered copying, of a work is very likely. There may also be some commercial dealing with the work by someone who claims they do not have the necessary knowledge that the work was an infringing work. The fair dealing permitted acts may be relevant, particularly in relation to criticism and review or reporting current events. You should be aware of the scope of the fair dealing provisions.

◼ Sample question

Could you answer this question? Below is a typical essay question that could arise on this topic. Guidelines on answering the question are included at the end of this chapter, whilst a sample problem question and guidance on tackling it can be found on the companion website.

ESSAY QUESTION

In *Designers Guild Ltd* v *Russell Williams (Textiles) Ltd* [2001] FSR 11, Lord Hoffmann said at para. 26:

'Generally speaking, in cases of artistic copyright, the more abstract and simple the copied idea, the less likely it is to constitute a substantial part. Originality, in the sense of the contribution of the author's skill and labour, tends to lie in the detail with which the basic idea is presented. Copyright law protects foxes better than hedgehogs.'

Discuss this statement in relation to what constitutes a substantial part of a work for the purposes of infringement.

◼ Copyright infringement

The acts restricted by copyright

Copyright is the exclusive right given to the owner to copy the work, or do any of the restricted acts in relation to the whole or a substantial part of the work.

KEY STATUTE

Section 16(1) and (2) Copyright, Designs and Patents Act 1988

The owner of the copyright in a work has the exclusive right to copy, issue copies of the work, rent, lend, perform, show, play or communicate the work to the public. The owner also has the right to make an adaptation of the work or do any of the above acts in relation to an adaptation.

Copyright in a work is infringed by a person who without the licence of the copyright owner does, or authorises another to do, any of the acts restricted by copyright in relation to the whole or a substantial part of the work.

The owner may grant a licence to another to do any of these restricted acts.

Authorisation

It is an infringement not only to perform one of the restricted acts but also to **authorise** another to do so. In other jurisdictions libraries have been held to have authorised copyright infringement by providing photocopiers without any warnings to the users or supervision against copyright infringement. However, in the UK merely making copying equipment available will only amount to authorisation if there has actually been some encouragement or at least turning a blind eye to infringement.

KEY DEFINITION: Authorise

To 'authorise' means to grant or purport to grant to a third person the right to do the act complained of.

KEY CASE

CBS Songs Ltd v *Amstrad Consumer Electronics plc* **[1988] 1 AC 1013, HL**

Concerning: whether providing machines which could be used for copyright infringement was authorising infringement

Facts

Amstrad was held not to be authorising copyright infringement by the sale of its twin-deck tape recorder machines which could be used to copy music, thereby infringing its copyright.

Legal principle

Merely facilitating unauthorised copying was not authorisation if the machines could be used for legitimate purposes.

Amstrad had not authorised the infringement even though their machines may have facilitated it. They had conferred a power but not a right to copy. This question is relevant to file-to-file sharing and the question should now be, did they actively encourage infringement or turn a blind eye when a reasonable person would think that infringement was likely to take place? In *Twentieth Century Fox Film Corp* v *Newzbin Ltd* authorisation was found when the copying and downloading of films was sanctioned and approved by an internet service provider.

Substantial part and indirect infringement

If an article such as a drawer is made according to a drawing, unauthorised copies of the drawer will indirectly infringe the copyright subsisting in the drawing. Not only copying the whole, but also copying a substantial amount of the work, will amount to infringement.

KEY STATUTE

Section 16(3) Copyright, Designs and Patents Act 1988

Copying must be in relation to the whole or any substantial part of the work and can be direct or indirect. It is immaterial whether any intervening acts themselves infringe.

It can be difficult to determine what a substantial amount is. There are no guidelines in the Act and different types of work are treated differently. Substantial must be decided by the quality of what has been taken rather than the quantity. If what has been copied is commonplace (see Chapter 7), an idea or fact, it will not normally be regarded as original enough to amount to a substantial part. However, taking part of a compilation of unoriginal material where there has been a substantial exercise of skill or judgement of the person creating the compilation may be substantial taking. A small portion of a work, if the most memorable or valuable part, such as the hook in a piece of music, can be substantial.

! Don't be tempted to . . .

Don't forget that when determining infringement by taking a substantial part, the method is to first identify the parts taken by the defendant, *then* isolate them from the remainder of the defendant's work, and *only then* consider whether those parts represent a substantial part of the claimant's work (*not the defendant's work*).

Imagine I reproduce the smile of the *Mona Lisa* (pretend it is still in copyright). I use the smile as a small portion of my work. To decide whether I have taken a substantial part of Leonardo da Vinci's work, look at how memorable a part the smile is and how important it is to da Vinci's work, not how important it is to mine. Keep in mind that if the defendant is competing with the claimant, this could be taken into account.

✎ EXAM TIP

Point out that if the courts concentrate on quality to determine substantiality they may end up demanding merit of the copyright work, and for original works no merit is required.

The importance of the work cannot be the test for all works. With computer programs a very minor piece of punctuation such as a full stop that took little skill or judgement to create may be important, in that the software will not work without it. It does not mean that copying that full stop is taking a substantial part of the whole program.

📖 REVISION NOTE

For a discussion of the quality requirements of copyright works please refer to Chapter 1.

If there has been regular cumulative copying of trivial amounts of a series of works, this cannot amount to a substantial part. Whether what has been taken is trivial may depend on how you look at the work itself. Small extracts taken from magazine articles where the typographical arrangement has been copied would be regarded as trivial if the 'work' is regarded as the whole magazine rather than each individual article within the magazine. However, copying even parts of sentences, if they encapsulate the author's intellectual creation, may infringe (see Derclaye, 2010). On the other hand, an accumulation of copies of parts of a work may infringe if, collectively, they represent a substantial part of the work (cf. infringing the database right by the extraction and/or reutilisation of insubstantial parts of the content of a database: see Chapter 11 on the database right).

Copying

What amounts to copying varies depending on the nature of the work in question.

KEY STATUTE

Section 17 Copyright, Designs and Patents Act 1988

Copying, in relation to a literary, dramatic, musical or artistic work, means reproducing the work in any material form including storing the work in any medium by electronic means. Copying an artistic work includes making a copy of a two-dimensional work in three dimensions and vice versa, or making a photograph of the whole or any substantial part of a film or broadcast. Copying of all types of work includes the making of copies which are transient or incidental to some other use of the work.

Consequently, unauthorised recording of any works of copyright by any method, even if transient or incidental, will infringe. Taking a single photograph of a substantial part of one frame of a film or an internet webpage infringes copyright. However, 'dimensional shift' or making a three-dimensional work out of a two-dimensional work applies only to artistic works. If a knitting pattern – a literary work – is made into a jumper – a three-dimensional object – there will be no copying. Infringement will, however, occur where actors in three dimensions enact a two-dimensional cartoon.

Causal connection

If two people each independently take a photograph of Buckingham Palace, even though the photographs may look identical there is no copying. To show infringement the claimant must first prove that the defendant has copied either consciously or unconsciously. They must show prior access to the copyright work. Once this is proved, the burden of proof shifts to the defendant, who must then give an explanation of why there are similarities between the works.

Mention that many creators include an 'accidental' mistake in their work. If the work is copied, the presence of the 'mistake' in their work will be very difficult if not impossible for the defendant to explain.

Altered copying

If the defendant has copied the whole of a work there is little problem apart from proof. If there have been considerable alterations it is more difficult to prove infringement. The court has to decide whether the defendant's work incorporates a substantial part of the skill and labour involved in the creation of the claimant's work.

KEY CASE

Designers Guild Ltd v *Russell Williams Textiles Ltd* **[2001] FSR 11, HL**
Concerning: altered copying

Facts

The claimant successfully sued for infringement of the copyright in an impressionistic fabric design comprising stripes with flowers scattered around the design. The defendant created a design based on a similar idea of stripes and scattered flowers. It looked very similar but there were many differences.

Legal principle

The test is whether the infringer had incorporated a substantial amount of the independent skill and labour of the author. You must look at the claimant's work and the importance and the amount of the work taken from that, not the importance of it to the work of the defendant. The cumulative effect of those similarities ought to be considered, but ideas or commonplace things will not be included.

✓ Make your answer stand out

The idea/expression debate is a long-standing one in the field of copyright. Ronan Deazley (2004) considers two House of Lords cases on what constitutes a substantial part. Make your answer stand out by explaining that Deazley discusses the idea/expression debate and asks whether the balance is weighted too much in favour of the author with the potential that creativity by others will be inhibited.

Issuing copies of the work to the public

This concerns **exhaustion of rights** and the free movement of goods within the **European Economic Area (EEA)**. It applies to all categories of works.

KEY STATUTE

Section 18 Copyright, Designs and Patents Act 1988

Issuing copies of the work to the public includes putting them into circulation in the EEA when copies have not previously been put into circulation there by or with the consent of the copyright owner, or outside the EEA when copies have not previously been put into circulation in the EEA or elsewhere.

Issuing to the public does not include subsequent distribution, sale, hiring or loan of copies previously put into circulation in the EEA or subsequent importation of such copies into the UK or another EEA state.

Consequently, the copyright owner can take action against anyone who for the first time issues a copy of their work to the public anywhere without their consent. They lose control over any copies once they put them into circulation in the EEA. If they first issued the copy in France or another EEA country but not the UK, they cannot prevent someone importing a copy from France into the UK and selling it. If they first issue the copy in the USA they can prevent its importation into the EEA. It should be noted that this right to issue applies to each and every copy of the work.

Rental or lending of work to the public

The right applies to the 'original' works of copyright (other than works of architecture in the form of a building or model for a building or a work of 'applied art'), films and sound recordings. The rental or lending of the DVDs or CDs (unless done privately) after the owner has issued them to the public gives rise to a right to obtain a royalty.

KEY STATUTE

Section 18A Copyright, Designs and Patents Act 1988

Rental is making a copy of the work available for use, on terms that it will or may be returned, for direct or indirect economic or commercial advantage.

Lending is making a copy of the work available for use, on terms that it will or may be returned, otherwise than for direct or indirect economic or commercial advantage, through an establishment which is accessible to the public.

Where an author of an original work agrees to its inclusion in a film, it is assumed that the author has assigned their rental rights in relation to that film and instead acquires a right to an equitable remuneration.

Performance, showing or playing of a work in public

The restricted act of performance applies to literary, dramatic or musical works. It does not apply to artistic works. The restricted act of playing or showing a work in public applies to sound recordings, films or broadcasts.

KEY STATUTE

Section 19(2) and (3) Copyright, Designs and Patents Act 1988

A performance includes the delivery of lectures, addresses, speeches and sermons and includes any mode of visual or acoustic presentation, including presentation by means of a sound recording, film or broadcast.

The playing or showing of the work in public is an act restricted by the copyright in a sound recording, film or broadcast.

The person in charge of the equipment used in playing music to members of the public, for example background music in a café, is the one infringing. A 'blanket' licence to allow such use may be obtained from the Performing Right Society.

What amounts to 'in public'?

A performance will be regarded as a public performance unless the audience is of a domestic nature. If payment is made there is no doubt that this will involve performance in public. In relation to the act of communication to the public, the Court of Justice of the European Union (CJEU) has held that guests in hotel bedrooms were considered to be part of the public and the transmission of signals to the television sets in the bedrooms fell within the restricted act (*Sociedad General de Autores y Editores de España (SGAE)* v *Rafael Hoteles SA*). The same principle should also apply to the restricted act of performing, showing or playing in public.

Communication to the public

This is a restricted act in relation to the original works, a sound recording, film or broadcast.

KEY STATUTE

Section 20 Copyright, Designs and Patents Act 1988

Communication to the public applies to original works, sound recordings, films and broadcasts and means communication to the public by electronic transmission including the broadcasting of the work or making available to the public by electronic transmission in such a way that the public can access it from a place and at a time individually chosen by them.

Despite having the authority to distribute hard copies of a work, placing a work on a website or providing a hypertext link to it without authority will infringe if the work is downloaded by any member of the public in the UK. It does not matter where the computer on which the website is hosted is physically located. Communication to the public will also include the retransmission of a terrestrial TV broadcast via the internet.

Making an adaptation

The restricted act only applies to literary, dramatic and musical works. Artistic works are not covered by the act of making an adaptation.

> **📖 REVISION NOTE**
>
> When an adaptation is made the economic rights are affected but moral rights of the author may also be infringed. (Please refer to Chapter 2 on this issue.)

> **KEY STATUTE**
>
> **Section 21(3) Copyright, Designs and Patents Act 1988**
>
> Adaptation in relation to a literary or dramatic work means translation, conversion of a dramatic work into a non-dramatic work or vice versa, or a version of a work in which the story or action is conveyed wholly or mainly by means of pictures into a form suitable to be reproduced in a book or periodical. In relation to a musical work it is an arrangement or transcription of the work. For a computer program or database, adaptation means an arrangement or altered version of it or a translation of it.

> **📖 REVISION NOTE**
>
> See Chapter 1 for discussion of adaptation of musical works and *Hyperion Records* v *Sawkins*.

Adaptation would include a substantial amount of a book that has been made into a play or translated, for example, from French to English. It covers an adaptation of an adaptation. If enough skill and judgement has been involved in the adaptation it may attract its own copyright, but would infringe the first work if done without the consent of its owner. Adaptation does not apply to an artistic work, so an artistic work can be infringed by copying but cannot be infringed by making an adaptation, per se.

■ Secondary infringements of copyright

Secondary infringement is all about commercial 'dealing' with infringing copies. It includes providing premises for the performance of, apparatus for making or transmitting an infringing article in the course of a business. Secondary and primary infringement does not have to have been committed by the same person. For a secondary infringement the person responsible must have knowledge or reason to believe that the copies are infringing copies and that what they are doing involves a secondary infringement.

KEY STATUTE

Sections 22–26 Copyright, Designs and Patents Act 1988

Copyright is infringed by importing, possessing or 'dealing' with, selling, letting for hire, offering or exposing for sale or hire, exhibiting or distributing an infringing copy in the course of a business and in a way as to affect prejudicially the owner of the copyright. Also by permitting the use of premises or supplying the apparatus for an infringing performance knowing or having reason to believe that secondary infringement will occur.

The main issue here is the knowledge needed by the secondary infringer.

KEY CASE

LA Gear Inc. v *Hi-Tec Sports plc* [1992] FSR 121, CA

Concerning: the meaning of 'has reason to believe' for secondary infringement

Facts

An employee of LA Gear had made a drawing for a sports shoe. It was later discovered that an identical shoe had been made by Hi-Tec Sports. Sending the defendant copies of the drawings and a letter saying they had copyright in them was held enough to make the defendant 'have reason to believe' the shoes were infringing the claimant's copyright.

Legal principle

The test must be objective: whether the reasonable man, with knowledge of the facts known to the defendant, would have formed the belief that the item was an infringing copy.

A 'reason to believe' would include a reasonable belief that the copyright had expired, did not subsist in the work, or that the copies had been made with the copyright owner's permission. Some of the criminal offences provided for under the 1988 Act closely follow the equivalent secondary infringements, and the same level of knowledge is required (that is, objective knowledge will suffice). The maximum penalty for some of the copyright offences is imprisonment for up to ten years and/or a fine. The criminal offences are set out in section 107 of the Act.

■ Remedies for infringement of copyright

The remedies applicable to civil infringement include injunctions, damages or an account of profits, delivery up and destruction orders. A maximum term of ten years' imprisonment is available for criminal offences. If there is a very strong case to suspect copyright infringement and a likelihood of serious damage, the copyright owner (or licensee) should apply for a search order. Such an order will be granted if it is necessary to prevent the destruction of the evidence.

Damages

Damages are awarded, if not too remote, in order to compensate the copyright owner for any actual loss suffered. These may be based on a likely royalty or lost sales. Liability of the defendant is strict for the 'primary' infringements but damages will not be awarded against the defendant if they did not know, and had no reason to believe, that copyright subsisted in the work.

> ✎ **EXAM TIP**
>
> Point out that a wise copyright owner will apply a prominent copyright notice to copies of their work so that infringers cannot claim to be ignorant of the subsistence of copyright in the work.

In assessing damages where the defendant knew or had reasonable grounds for knowing that they engaged in infringing activity, the damages awarded shall be appropriate to the actual damage suffered by the claimant. All appropriate aspects shall be taken into account, in particular, the negative economic aspects, including lost profits suffered by the claimant or any unfair profits made by the defendant and elements other than economic factors including moral prejudice caused to the claimant. Where appropriate, damages may be assessed on the basis of royalties or fees which would have been due had the defendant obtained a licence to perform the acts in question. This method of calculating damages (which, arguably, restates previous practice) applies to all forms of intellectual property rights, not just copyright, and are provided for by reg. 3 of the Intellectual Property (Enforcement, etc.) Regulations 2006, implementing the Directive on the enforcement of intellectual property rights.

Injunctions

An **injunction** may order a person to stop making infringing copies or to destroy something which is used for making infringing copies. Injunctions are equitable and therefore discretionary. The court must feel that there is a serious issue to be tried. Injunctions are unlikely to be granted if damages would be an adequate remedy. However, they are a very common form of protection in this area of law. Quick action often needs to be taken and it may be many years before an action would come to full trial. The court will consider on the balance of convenience the impact of granting or refusing the injunction on each of the parties.

> **KEY DEFINITION: Injunction**
>
> An injunction is an order of the court which prohibits an act or the commencement or continuance of an act. Alternatively, an injunction might order a person to perform some act.

Section 97A provides for a special form of injunction to be imposed on service providers where they have actual knowledge that a person is using their service to infringe copyright. In determining whether a service provider has actual knowledge, account is to be taken of all matters relevant in the particular circumstance including whether the service provider has received an appropriate notice.

Account of profits

An account of profits is intended to prevent unjust enrichment. That is the gain made by the defendant due to the infringement, not the retail value of the infringing articles. An account may be very difficult to assess. However, it may be the only monetary remedy obtainable when damages are unavailable because the defendant did not have reason to believe that copyright subsisted in the work.

Additional damages

Additional damages may be awarded having regard to all the circumstances, in particular, the flagrancy of the infringement and the benefit accruing to the defendant. The House of Lords (now the Supreme Court) confirmed in *Redrow Homes* v *Betts Brothers plc* that they may only be claimed with ordinary damages but not with a claim for an account of profits. However, this must now be seen in the context of the Directive on the enforcement of intellectual property rights (see above).

Delivery up

A court may order that infringing copies, or articles designed or adapted for making copies of the copyright owner's work, are delivered up to them. The person must know or have reason to believe that the article has been or is to be used to make infringing copies. An order for the disposal of the infringing copies must also be made.

A new approach to online infringement?

The Digital Economy Act 2010 provides for a means of tackling the problem of online infringement by serial infringers. Copyright owners may send a Copyright Infringement

Report (CIR) to a service provider where the owner suspects a subscriber to the service has used it to infringe their copyright. The service provider then notifies the subscriber. From time to time, copyright owners may be sent copyright infringement lists. Where it appears that a subscriber has reached a threshold limit (to be set by a code), the copyright owner may apply to the court for an order identifying the subscriber and then may bring proceedings against the subscriber. It appears at this stage that a 'three-strikes' in 12 months test may apply before triggering a court order identifying the subscriber alleged to be infringing the owner's copyright.

■ Defences to copyright infringement and the permitted acts

There are some defences to copyright infringement which are not expressly provided for in the Act. They include a public interest defence. Acquiescence or implied authorisation may also be at issue. Delay in asserting a right may disentitle the owner to royalties for past acts, as in *Fisher* v *Brooker* (discussed in Chapter 2). A defendant may argue that they have not taken a substantial part of the copyright work or that copyright does not subsist in the work.

Numerous '**permitted acts**' are included in the Act. These are wide-ranging and include fair dealing, making temporary copies (for example, for onward transmission where there is no independent economic significance), making accessible copies for visually impaired persons, certain uses by educational establishments, libraries and archives, in relation to computer programs and databases, for public administration purposes and a great many miscellaneous exceptions, including time-shifting. Format shifting, for example, where a person has a legitimate copy on a CD and wishes to make a copy on to an MP3 player for their own private use is not yet permitted but will be in the future. There will also be an exception to cover parodies. Some new permitted acts and other issues affecting intellectual property rights were proposed in the Gowers Review and the Hargreaves Report.

> **✎ EXAM TIP**
>
> Make sure you are aware of and can discuss proposals for changes to copyright law, including important reports and developments at the European and international level. This applies also to all the other intellectual property rights.

Public interest

Cases where the public interest is at issue often concern the publication of information, and frequently questions of confidence will be raised.

📖 REVISION NOTE

Please see Chapter 4 on confidentiality.

The defence of public interest does not claim that there is no copyright subsisting in the work but that it is not in the public interest to enforce the right. This could be used where a work was immoral or in some way in contravention to society's values. It needs to be balanced against the right to freedom of expression which exists under the Human Rights Act 1998.

KEY CASE

Hyde Park Residence Ltd v Yelland [2000] RPC 604, CA

Concerning: whether the public interest defence applied to copyright infringement

Facts

The day before Diana, Princess of Wales, and Dodi Al Fayed were killed in a car crash they had been recorded on video at a Paris property, with the time of their arrival and departure displayed. Stills from the video were made and published in *The Sun* newspaper to show that Mr Mohamed Al Fayed had lied about the duration of the visit. When sued for copyright infringement, *The Sun* failed in the defences of public interest and fair dealing for the purpose of reporting current events.

Legal principle

If information of interest contained within the work (the times of arrival and departure) could have been made available without infringing copyright, publication would not be necessary and the public interest defence would be unavailable.

Although the court must have regard to the right of freedom of expression, there will be no justification for copyright infringement if the necessary facts could be disclosed without such infringement.

The permitted acts

The justification for these permitted acts is that it provides a fair balance between the rights of the copyright owner and the rights of society at large. They cover such things as education, libraries and archives. In these circumstances there will have been an infringement of a work, but the copyright owner's commercial exploitation of the work is deemed not to have been unduly harmed. Of particular relevance for students are the fair dealing provisions.

Fair dealing

Fair dealing covers non-commercial research or private study, criticism, review and reporting current events. If the part taken is not substantial, then there is no infringement of copyright and no need to rely on the permitted acts. You must consider the number, extent and proportions of any quotations. Long extracts and short comments may be unfair. If the use made of them is for comment, criticism or review, that may be fair dealing. If they are used for a rival purpose, they may be unfair. But it must be a matter of impression of whether it would seriously prejudice the commercial value of the copyright work. If the work has not been published, dealing with it is unlikely to be fair.

> ✎ **EXAM TIP**
>
> Note that an injunction will rarely be granted if the defendant has an arguable defence of fair dealing. This is to protect freedom of speech. Highly relevant to the press and politics.

Research or private study, section 29

This applies to the original works (subject to a limitation for computer programs which have their own specific permitted acts) and typographical arrangements. The research must be for non-commercial purposes. There is a requirement that a sufficient acknowledgement be made, the name of the author and title of the work. The research must be to facilitate the person's own research, not another's. So providing study notes for others would not be included. This exception is to be extended to cover the copying of sound recordings, films and broadcasts.

Criticism, review and reporting current events, section 30

The section applies to works or the performance of a work. The criticism or review must be accompanied by a sufficient acknowledgement. It will only be available if the work has been made available to the public. The criticism or review does not need to be the only purpose for using the work, provided it was a significant purpose. The criticism does not have to be of the work itself but can be directed at another work. A television programme (the work) can be used to comment on the use of 'chequebook' journalism (another work). It is proposed that this section be expanded to state that it will not be infringement to use a quotation from a copyright work for purposes such as criticism or review as long as the use is justified, fair and the source acknowledged.

In reporting current events, the event involved does not have to be recent but must comment on other events which are of current interest. So an old video of Princess Diana could be used to comment upon a current event such as the inquest into her death. It does not apply to photographs. No acknowledgement is needed in the case of reporting current events by means of a sound recording, film or broadcast where this would be impossible for reasons of practicability or otherwise.

> ✓ **Make your answer stand out**
>
> To get good marks you must show that you are aware of proposed reforms in this area under the Enterprise and Regulatory Reform Act 2013. A private copying exception is to be introduced as well as a right to parody as long as it is fair. Data mining for non-commercial purposes will be allowed. There will be a new licensing scheme to cover orphan works, use of which will be permitted if the prospective user has made a diligent search for the owner and they cannot be found. A royalty will be paid to the authorising body. Collecting societies will be permitted to operate a voluntary but opt-out collective licensing scheme.

■ Putting it all together

Answer guidelines

See the essay question at the start of the chapter.

Approaching the question

This question involves a longish quote. Be careful how you interpret it. Do not take an overly literal approach but consider the general gist.

Important points to include

- First note that, under section 16(3) Copyright, Designs and Patents Act 1988, infringement requires that the relevant restricted act has to be carried out in relation to the whole or a substantial part of the work.
- Note that it is the quality of the part taken rather than its quantity that is important.
- Mention that when testing for infringement, comparison should be made between the part taken and the claimant's work rather than the defendant's work.
- Deal with Lord Hoffmann's statement – you could usefully introduce cases such as *Kenrick* v *Lawrence* here which is a good example of what he was thinking about.

✓ Make your answer stand out

It would help to mention something about the policy of copyright protection. For example, if ideas are expressed with little detail, there is the difficulty of deciding whether there has been copying, if denied. Also, copyright would be in danger of protecting ideas rather than expression.

READ TO IMPRESS

Deazley, R. (2004) 'Copyright in the House of Lords: recent cases, juridical reasoning and academic writing', 2 *Intellectual Property Quarterly*, 121.

Derclaye, E. (2010) '*Infopaq International A/S* v *Danske Dagblades Forening* (C-5/08): wonderful or worrisome? The impact of the ECJ ruling in *Infopaq* on UK copyright law', 32(5) *EIPR*, 247.

Heath-Saunders, A. (2005) 'It's a fair copy: the defence of fair dealing in cases of copyright infringement', June, *Corporate Briefing*, 8.

Rahmatian, A. (2012) *Temple Island Collections* v *New English Teas*' 34(11) *EIPR*, 796

Sims, A. (2006) 'The public interest defence in copyright: myth or reality?', 28(6) *EIPR*, 335.

Spencer, M. (2005) 'Vagueness in the scope of copyright', 121 *LQR*, 657.

Stephens, K. (2006) 'Copyright: non-textual infringement', 35(5) *Chartered Institute of Patent Agents Journal*, 356.

www.pearsoned.co.uk/lawexpress

Go online to access more revision support including quizzes to test your knowledge, sample questions with answer guidelines, podcasts you can download, and more!

Confidentiality

4

■ Topic map

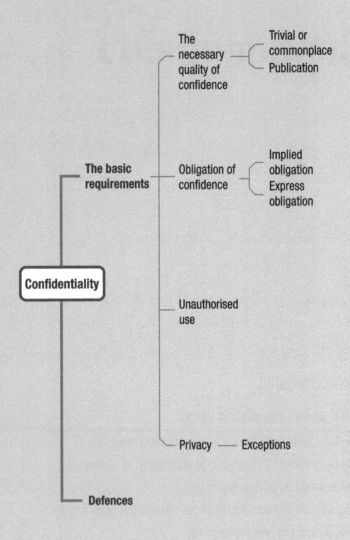

■ Introduction

If you say that you will keep a secret, then you must.

If you acquire secret information in confidence you may use it only for the purposes for which it was given to you. Confidential information may be personal, commercial, industrial or governmental. Such information is not restricted to the written or spoken word but may also include images and ideas. This is a very difficult area of law and, although an obligation of confidence may arise in contract, much is implied by the principles of equity. It is judge-made law and, although benefiting from flexibility, many of the cases contradict each other. However, for information to be regarded as confidential it must have the necessary quality of confidence about it. No one will be prevented from using truthful information or reverse engineering manufactured products that are already in the public domain. You cannot impose a secret on someone. In addition, you cannot stop an employee using their skill and know-how in order to gain future employment, but you may obtain an injunction to prevent them from divulging trade secrets or acting in breach of their duty of fidelity. Although there is no fundamental right of privacy in English law, the law of confidence, combined with the Human Rights Act 1998 and with Articles 8 and 10 of the European Convention for the Protection of Human Rights and Fundamental Freedoms, can protect the right of privacy subject to disclosure in the public interest.

ASSESSMENT ADVICE

Essay questions

Essay questions on this topic may well ask you to follow developments in this flexible area of law. This could involve discussion of commercial secrets and the development of the 'springboard' doctrine with the subsequent decision that, rather than granting an injunction, damages are an adequate remedy. You may also be asked to analyse the changing nature of private information due to the advent of the Human Rights Act.

Problem questions

Problem questions may well involve difficult areas, such as when an innocent third party receives confidential information without realising its confidential nature or when eavesdropping occurs. There may also be a problem that involves the 'kiss and tell' type of story or where an ex-partner or ex-employee sells the story or writes a book depicting their time in the company/employment of a celebrity.

Sample question

Could you answer this question? Below is a typical problem question that could arise on this topic. Guidelines on answering the question are included at the end of this chapter, whilst a sample essay question and guidance on tackling it can be found on the companion website.

PROBLEM QUESTION

Liz is a jazz singer. She has had considerable success but has always been a private person and has not encouraged publicity. For many years she was in daily contact with Olive, with whom she went to school. Olive was her best friend and confidante. Olive helped Liz overcome depression after she divorced her husband due to his adultery, and it was Olive who helped her come to terms with the fact that she had Parkinson's disease (a progressive neurological condition that affects walking, talking and writing). Olive accompanied Liz on all the singing tours she made between 1992 and 2005, eating together every evening, meeting all her friends and generally sharing her life. In 2004 the relationship between the two women grew strained, culminating in a very bad argument. They have not spoken for two years. Liz has discovered that Olive has written a book about their friendship which is about to be published. Liz became aware of the book following enquiries she made after she was startled by one photographer taking a photograph of her walking along the street and another climbing on to the wall of her garden so that he could take photographs of her sunbathing.

Both photographs of Liz have been sold to newspapers, which are about to publish them. Olive says that the book is not about Liz but about her own life during the period of 1992–2005 and Liz cannot prevent its publication.

Advise Liz on whether she can prevent the publication of the book and the photographs.

The basic requirements

KEY CASE

Coco v *A.N. Clark (Engineers) Ltd* [1969] RPC 41, ChD

Concerning: basic requirements for liability

Facts

Marco Paolo Coco designed a moped engine. He entered into negotiations with Clark to manufacture the engine but these negotiations broke down. No contract was involved. Clark produced a similar moped engine, which Coco unsuccessfully claimed was based on his engine.

> **Legal principle**
>
> 1. The information must have the necessary quality of confidence about it.
>
> 2. The information must have been imparted in circumstances imposing an obligation of confidence.
>
> 3. There must be an unauthorised use of that information to the detriment of the party communicating it.

The necessary quality of confidence

Trivial or commonplace

In order to be held to be confidential, information must not be trivial or commonplace, in the public domain or too vague. It does not have to be particularly special information, and simple things such as lists of customers or an original combination of ideas can be regarded as confidential. **Trade secrets**, however, are given far stronger protection. There is unfortunately no legal definition of trade secrets.

KEY CASE

> *Faccenda Chicken Ltd* v *Fowler* **[1986] 1 All ER 617, CA**
>
> *Concerning: an ex-employee taking sales information*
>
> **Facts**
>
> An employee left his employment with know-how concerning the fresh chicken trade of his employer. He started up in competition using this know-how.
>
> **Legal principle**
>
> Trivial information, easily accessible information and employee know-how are not protected as trade secrets. Trade secrets are so confidential that there is a duty even without a contractual agreement to keep them secret after the end of the employment relationship.

KEY DEFINITION: Trade secret

> A trade secret is information that would cause real harm if it were disclosed to a competitor and the owner had limited its dissemination.

Some duties of confidence, such as that of an employee and employer, although expressed in a contract of employment, are also implied by law. The implied duty of ex-employees is far less onerous than that of present employees and covers only trade secrets, unless protected by a specific contractual term.

> ! **Don't be tempted to . . .**
>
> Don't forget that it may be *implied* that an employee should keep their employer's secrets. There is a balance required between the need of employees to work using the know-how and experience gained through their employment and the need for the employer to protect their sensitive information from being dispersed to rivals.

To determine whether the information is to be regarded as a trade secret one must look at the nature of the employment: would the employee routinely handle confidential information? The nature of the information itself: would it be easily available to the public? Whether the employer impressed upon the employee the confidentiality of the information and, in addition, whether the information can be easily isolated from other information the employee is free to disclose are important issues to be considered. Where a person is involved in work which would result in an invention being made, this normally would be classed as a trade secret.

Publication

If information is in the public domain, it will no longer be confidential and its use can no longer be prevented. In the past, if the person whose conscience was fixed by the confidence put the information in the public domain themselves, they could, for a period of time, be prevented by an injunction from using the information to the detriment of the owner. This was intended to stop a person from benefiting from their own wrong. Today however, damages are felt to be a more appropriate remedy.

Obligation of confidence

The information must have been imparted in circumstances importing an obligation of confidence. The party receiving the information must have their conscience fixed in equity. This can either be by contract, by oral agreement, or implied by law. The test can be subjective – was it assumed by the parties that the disclosure was in confidence? – or objective – would other reasonable people assume the information had been imparted in confidence? If no one would reasonably think that the circumstance could give rise to a confidence, then it will not.

> ! **Don't be tempted to . . .**
>
> Don't forget to consider the problem of eavesdropping. It is uncertain whether an obligation arises in such circumstances, as the information has not been imparted in circumstances importing an obligation of confidence, as required in *Coco* v *Clark*.

Implied obligation

By using such methods as encryption when selling goods you are making information difficult to access or reverse-engineer, as well as letting people know that you do not want them to access your secret information. Does this mean that their conscience is fixed in equity? This can be problematic, for without a contractual agreement there is no consent on the behalf of the purchaser and a confider cannot impose an obligation of confidence upon another. Encrypting data tends to indicate that the owner of the data does not want others to access the raw data rather than imposing an obligation of confidence on members of the public who have possession of the products.

✎ EXAM TIP

It is worth pointing out that as technology improves it is much easier for people to gain access to confidential material but that the circumstances importing an obligation of confidence may not exist. Make sure you stress the flexibility offered by the law of confidence. We can see the benefits of it being able to adapt, demonstrated in *Douglas v Hello! (No. 6)* where it was accepted that taking photographs surreptitiously was a breach of confidence.

KEY CASE

Michael Douglas v *Hello! Ltd (No. 6)* [2006] QB 125, CA

Concerning: whether unauthorised photographs were taken in breach of a duty of confidence

Facts

A photographer, despite heavy security, surreptitiously took photographs of a celebrity wedding. The photographs were published in the magazine *Hello!* and the celebrities sued the magazine for breach of confidence.

Legal principle

Making it clear that photographs should not be taken, together with strict security measures, can give rise to a duty of confidence.

Keep in mind that this was not a commercial situation but a case of private information where the parties had a reasonable expectation of privacy. The fact that the photographer had not agreed to be bound was irrelevant as he knew that the information was reasonably regarded by the couple as confidential.

Express obligation

Restrictive covenants can be included in the contract of employment and these will protect the employer even after the employment relationship has ended. They should not, however, be drafted too widely in either length or width, or the courts will find them unenforceable.

The court will not rewrite a clause on behalf of the employer. Neither will they uphold a covenant that goes beyond the protection necessary for trade secrets: for instance, in an attempt to prevent competition or prevent the ex-employee using their skill and knowledge for a new employer or on his own behalf.

> **! Don't be tempted to . . .**
>
> Don't think that the position of third parties receiving confidential information is clear-cut. If a third party receives information knowing it to be confidential or in circumstances where a reasonable person would assume that the information is confidential, they too will be bound. If, however, they only later discover the confidential nature of the information, they may be under an obligation from the time they become aware of its nature and their conscience will then become fixed. However, if the innocent third party has not agreed to be bound, it would seem not to comply with the guidance in *Coco* v *Clark*, that the information must have been imparted in circumstances imposing an obligation of confidence.

Unauthorised use

The use must be detrimental to the party that communicated it. This can be economic damage or where there is harm to a person's social standing. It appears that it is not necessary that the defendant is aware that the use in question is in breach of confidence.

> **📖 REVISION NOTE**
>
> Confidential information is extremely important in the pre-filing stage of a patent application. However, disclosures in breach of confidence will not prejudice novelty for a limited period of time. Refer to Chapter 5 on patentability.

Privacy

There is no right of privacy in English law but, since the Human Rights Act 1998, Article 8 of the Convention for the Protection of Human Rights and Fundamental Freedoms has established that everyone has a right to respect for their private and family life, their home and correspondence. There is, however, a conflicting right in Article 10, the right to freedom of expression, and these rights can be at variance. Each of these Convention rights are subject to derogations, for example, in the case of national security or public safety.

> **KEY DEFINITION: Private information**
>
> Information or conduct, the disclosure of which would be highly offensive to a reasonable person of ordinary sensibilities.

KEY CASE

Campbell v *Mirror Group Newspapers* [2004] 2 All ER 995, HL

Concerning: misuse of private information and whether disclosure was in the public interest

Facts

Naomi Campbell, a 'supermodel', had claimed that she was not addicted to drugs. The *Mirror* newspaper published an article describing the treatment she was undergoing at Narcotics Anonymous and a photo of her coming out of a Narcotics Anonymous meeting.

Legal principle

By a majority decision, the court decided that a role model can be exposed for hypocrisy, consequently drug treatment after denial of addiction was open to exposure. However, there is still a 'reasonable expectation of privacy' and the photograph was not necessary in order to demonstrate that she had lied.

There must be a balance between a right to privacy and the right to freedom of expression. There is some information that has an obvious 'reasonable expectation of privacy'. It must of course be personal, the claimant must not have intended to share it with the general public, and such **private information** will include information on health, sexual orientation, intimate relationships and finances. The information will not be private if it is generally accessible or if it relates to a criminal act.

! **Don't be tempted to . . .**

Don't assume that photographs will be treated in the same way as other types of information. In *Campbell* the photographs taken in the street were held to be private and confidential. In a later case (concerning photographs taken in the street of the child of the author J.K. Rowling) the Court of Appeal said that privacy should be viewed from the perspective of a reasonable person of ordinary sensibilities placed in the same position. This interpretation seems to extend to matter that can be regarded as secret.

Exceptions

There are exceptions under the Human Rights Act 1998 in respect of, inter alia:

- national security;
- prevention of crime;
- protection of rights or freedoms of others or the reputation of others.

■ Defences

There are defences to a breach of confidence action such as justification, or fair comment. Confidential information will not be protected where there has been wrongdoing or inappropriate behaviour. An important defence to an accusation of breach of confidence is that the publication was made in the public interest. The breach was necessary to allow the wrongful behaviour to be discovered. Consequently, the public interest in the revelation of the information outweighs the claimant's right to confidentiality. But remember, just because information is of interest to the public does not mean it is in the public interest to know it. Also, some confidential relationships such as doctor/patient or solicitor/client are very important and disclosure would rarely be accepted as being justified. If, however, the disclosure was felt to be necessary, the information must only be disclosed to the appropriate authorities, never the newspapers.

✓ Make your answer stand out

The second requirement in *Coco* v *Clark*, that the information must have been imparted in circumstances imposing an obligation of confidence, has been in some cases circumvented in recent years. However, this does not seem to be universal. Make your answer stand out by showing that you understand that there also seems to be a difference between quality of confidence and the treatment of commercial and private information. Private information is protected if there is a reasonable expectation of privacy, but should commercial information be protected if a person knew or ought to have known that it was confidential in nature? (The answer is no.) For a discussion of this see Aplin (2007).

■ Putting it all together

Answer guidelines

See the problem question at the start of the chapter.

Approaching the question

When answering a problem question such as this you must identify the legal issues. You then apply the law to the fact situation. Be careful to distinguish between what is and what is not relevant and then give coherent, logical and persuasive advice.

Important points to include

- Liz can claim breach of confidence and an injunction in relation to the book and at least one of the photographs.
- Traditionally, under *Coco* v *Clark* confidential information:
  1. must have the necessary quality of confidence (not be trivial, commonplace or in the public domain);
  2. must be imparted in a situation imposing an obligation of confidence;
  3. must be subject to unauthorised use made by the party under the obligation.
- With private information, after *Campbell* and *Douglas* it is no longer necessary to have a confidential obligation imposed. There is now an assumption that if information is private it is also confidential.
- Information about health matters such as depression will be regarded as private, as would a husband's adultery, unless Liz openly quarrelled with her husband about it in public earshot.
- A confidential duty now arises where a person knows or ought to know that there was a reasonable expectation of privacy, so the information in the book would be private and confidential.
- Once the information is held to be private the courts will then balance Articles 8 and 10 of the Convention for the Protection of Human Rights and Fundamental Freedoms.
- Olive claims the book is about her life and she has a right to freedom of expression under Article 10. The court is likely to hold that Olive's experiences were only a reflection of Liz's life and Liz's right to privacy outweighed any right of Olive's.
- In *Campbell* photographs were held to be private and an injunction was granted, but here we must ask would Liz really have a reasonable expectation of privacy in walking along a public road, unlike in the walled garden?

✓ **Make your answer stand out**

Stress the fact that Liz did not talk about her life in public, that she had not exposed herself to media interest and that she was not held out as a role model. She had not behaved hypocritically as had Naomi Campbell. Just because she is famous, it does not mean the public have a right to know all about her.

READ TO IMPRESS

Aplin, T. (2007) 'Commercial confidences after the Human Rights Act', 29(10) *EIPR*, 411.

Brazell, L. (2005) 'Confidence, privacy and human rights: English law in the twenty-first century', 27(11) *EIPR*, 405.

Carty, H. (2008) 'An analysis of the modern action for breach of commercial confidence: when is protection merited?', 4 *Intellectual Property Quarterly*, 416.

Cran, D. and Joseph, P. (2011) 'Breach of confidence claims against ex-employees and consultants', 6(10) *Journal of Intellectual Property Law and Practice*, 688.

Lang, J. (2003) 'The protection of commercial trade secrets', 25(10) *EIPR*, 462.

www.pearsoned.co.uk/lawexpress

Go online to access more revision support including quizzes to test your knowledge, sample questions with answer guidelines, podcasts you can download, and more!

Patentability, entitlement and ownership

5

Revision checklist

Essential points you should know:

- [ ] What the basic requirements for the grant of a patent are
- [ ] What is meant by 'novelty'
- [ ] What will destroy novelty
- [ ] What an enabling disclosure is
- [ ] What constitutes an inventive step
- [ ] What material a skilled person should take into account when assessing inventive step
- [ ] What inventions are capable of industrial application
- [ ] What things are excluded from the meaning of invention
- [ ] Who is entitled to claim to be the inventor or owner of an invention

◼ Topic map

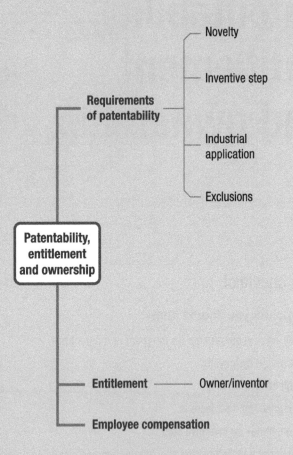

A printable version of this topic map is available from **www.pearsoned.co.uk/lawexpress**

■ Introduction

Ideas by themselves are not protectable but in some circumstances 'ideas' can be developed into a successful patent application.

Patents are granted for new, non-obvious product or process inventions that have an industrial application and which have not been excluded from patentability. On payment of a fee a patent gives the owner a monopoly in a particular territory, enabling them to exploit the invention exclusively for a period of up to 20 years. Although the inventor benefits from the patent in that they can work, sell or license it, society also benefits because not only is innovation encouraged but also the invention will eventually fall into the public domain when the patent expires.

ASSESSMENT ADVICE

Problem questions

There may be a problem question that incorporates patentability in your examination. Novelty may include issues of confidentiality and the date of filing. Inventive step may involve what appears to be a routine development rather than something completely new. The issue of industrial application may need some discussion about the actual construction of the claim. Sometimes the facts seem to be very scientific, which can appear daunting but, remember, you are not being asked to understand the science, you are being asked to apply the law. If you do this clearly and appropriately, you should gain a good mark.

It is very important to remember when talking about patents that there are significant policy issues involved in this area of law. There is an underlying intention that society will benefit in two ways: by the innovation that will be encouraged by a period of monopoly given to the owner of the patent, then ultimately because the invention will become available to be exploited for the use of all. However, there are exclusions to the grant of a patent. These exclusions are also made for policy reasons.

■ Sample question

Could you answer this question? Below is a typical essay question that could arise on this topic. Guidelines on answering the question are included at the end of this chapter, whilst a sample problem question and guidance on tackling it can be found on the companion website.

ESSAY QUESTION

The Patents Act 1977 contains no definition of what an invention is for the purposes of obtaining a patent, but a 'non-obvious advance in technology' would seem to be an adequate description.

Explain what an invention is and whether a 'non-obvious advance in technology' is a good definition.

■ Requirements for patentability

KEY STATUTE

Section 1 Patents Act 1977

'(1) A patent may be granted . . . if

    (a) the invention is new

    (b) it involves an inventive step

    (c) it is capable of industrial application

    (d) it is not excluded.'

A new invention means new to the public, so that secret use will not destroy novelty. 'An inventive step' is something that is not obvious to someone skilled in the art. 'Capable of industrial application' means that, no matter how clever it is, unless it is a product or process which has a function, there can be no patent granted. Finally, no patent will be granted for certain excluded inventions.

Novelty

KEY STATUTE

Section 2 Patents Act 1977

'An invention shall be new if it does not form part of the state of the art. The state of the art comprises all matter [whether a product, a process, information about either, or anything else] which has at any time before the priority date been made available to the public [whether in the United Kingdom or elsewhere] by written or oral description, by use or in any other way.'

Note: The state of the art also includes matter in an application for another patent with an earlier priority date published on or after the priority date of the invention at issue.

! Don't be tempted to . . .

Don't think that the state of the art is a narrow concept. To be new, the invention must not have been made available to the public in any way, anywhere in the world, at any time before the **priority date**. If it has been made available in this way, it will be part of the state of the art and cannot be new. There are problems in what constitutes the 'use' that needs to be made of the invention to amount to making it available to the public, so you should consider this carefully.

If something has been available to the public in the past, even if in a far-off country and a very long time ago, it will not be regarded as new for the purposes of section 1 of the Patents Act. However, assuming it is indeed new, if you reveal your invention before the **filing date** in any way, by telling people (or even one person) about it, by writing an article in a journal or by giving a talk at a conference, novelty will be destroyed and you will be unable to obtain a patent unless your disclosure was made in circumstances of confidence.

📖 **REVISION NOTE**

When considering novelty, remember that disclosures made in confidence will not become part of the state of the art. You should refer to Chapter 4 on confidentiality in relation to non-disclosure agreements.

KEY CASE

Lux Traffic Controls Ltd v *Pike Signals Ltd* **[1993] RPC 107, ChD**
Concerning: what use amounts to disclosure to the public

Facts

It was claimed that a temporary traffic signal was not 'new' because it had been made available to the public in a paper, by oral disclosure and by the use of a prototype which had been tested in public in Somerset.

Legal principle

A prior publication must contain clear and unmistakable directions to do what the patentee claims to have invented; a signpost will not suffice. Where prior use is concerned, there is no need for a skilled person actually to examine the invention as long as they were free in law and equity to do so, and if a skilled person had seen it they would have been able to understand what the inventive concept was.

In contrast to *Lux*, if the prototype had been displayed in private and the people who actually saw it did not understand what they were seeing, no disclosure would have taken place.

KEY DEFINITION: Skilled person

The skilled person is an unimaginative person, or team of uninventive people, with the common general knowledge available to a person in the field at the date of filing. They will only think the obvious and will not question general assumptions.

Note that a **skilled person** is needed to decide whether there has been disclosure, for they understand the **state of the art** in the area of the invention. They do not actually have to see or touch the invention for it to have become available to the public, but they must have been free in law or equity to have done so.

KEY CASE

Synthon v *SmithKline Beecham plc (No. 2)* [2006] RPC 10, HL
Concerning: the differing roles of the skilled person in relation to the concepts of disclosure and enablement

Facts

This was an appeal to the House of Lords by Synthon to revoke SmithKline's patent for an anti-depression drug. The application was based on the disclosure of Synthon's own flawed earlier patent application. SmithKline's patent was found to be invalid for lack of novelty based on section 2(3) of the Patents Act 1977.

Legal principle

What is regarded as part of the state of the art includes things disclosed to a skilled person which, if performed, must infringe the patent. To decide whether there was an *enabling* disclosure it is assumed that the skilled person would be willing to conduct trial and error experiments to get the invention to work. In other words, trial and error experiments are relevant to whether what has been disclosed is *enabled*. Trial and error experiments are not relevant, however, to the question of disclosure. Enablement and disclosure are two different concepts. As Lord Hoffmann said (at para 30):

'. . . in deciding whether there has been anticipation, there is a serious risk of confusion if the two requirements [disclosure and enablement] are not kept distinct . . . for the purpose of disclosure, the prior art must disclose an invention which, if performed, would necessarily infringe the patent. It is not enough to say that, given the prior art, the person skilled in the art would, without undue burden, be able to come up with an invention which infringed the patent. But once the very subject matter of the invention has been disclosed by the prior art and the question is whether it was enabled, the person skilled in the art is assumed to be willing to make trial and error experiments to get it to work. If, therefore, one asks whether some degree of experimentation is to be assumed, it is very important to know whether one is talking about disclosure or about enablement.'

✓ **Make your answer stand out**

Section 2(3) is intended to prevent double patenting by providing that matter in an unpublished patent application having an earlier priority date is taken into account and can be novelty-destroying. Make your answer stand out in a problem question where there had been an unpublished patent application to explain that you understand that this is why this section is applicable only to the issue of novelty and not to the question of obviousness. *Synthon* v *SmithKline Beecham plc* is an important case in this area and is discussed by Sharples and Curley (2006), explaining that to anticipate a patent the prior publication must disclose the invention and contain clear and unmistakable directions to do what the patentee claims to have invented; a signpost needing trial and error experimentation will not suffice. Reference to this article would make your answer stand out by displaying wider reading and allow you to demonstrate a depth of understanding on this issue.

Any disclosure which can anticipate an invention must be viewed by the unimaginative skilled reader at the time of the publication. It must not be viewed with hindsight taking into account the present invention. The prior disclosure must not just be an indication, a possibility or a signpost but *must* lead to the present invention. However, the skilled person may use their unimaginative skill and knowledge plus trial and error experiments to attempt to make the prior disclosure work (enablement). Consequently the skilled person in *Lux Traffic Controls* (above) could experiment by driving up to the traffic lights at different speeds in order to see how to trigger the change of lights. If by this experimentation they are *bound* to discover the inventive concept, it has been disclosed. Enablement is different. With enablement the skilled person must, from what was disclosed, be able to make the invention work, using unimaginative trial and error experiments etc., and not just understand what it is.

✎ **EXAM TIP**

Using headings when dealing with issues such as disclosure and enablement will ensure that you do not confuse them. Your reader will also understand that you know they are two separate concepts.

Inventive step

KEY STATUTE

Section 3 Patents Act 1977

'An invention shall be taken to involve an inventive step if it is not obvious to a person skilled in the art, having regard to any matter which forms part of the state of the art . . .'

To obtain a patent the invention must not only be new but it must also involve some invention or creative concept. This prevents a monopoly being created over things that are common general knowledge and should therefore be available for all to use.

! Don't be tempted to . . .

Don't forget to stress that an inventive step is not merely an obvious extension to what has gone before. It requires either the addition of a new idea to the existing stock of knowledge, or doing a new thing, achieving a goal or solving a problem. It is not possible to give a statutory definition of what constitutes an inventive step but guidelines have been established by the courts in the *Windsurfing* case (now restated as the *Pozzoli* test) to help in answering the question and you must be able to discuss these in detail.

KEY CASE

***Windsurfing International Inc.* v *Tabur Marine (CB) Ltd* [1985] RPC 59, CA**

Concerning: a structured way of approaching the problem of whether an invention is obvious to a person skilled in the art

Facts

The claimant had a patent for a windsurfing board and took action against the defendants for infringement of the patent. The defendants claimed that the patent should be revoked for invalidity as the invention had been anticipated in 1958 by a boy aged 12 who had used a similar sailboard while on a short holiday.

Legal principle

The court must identify the inventive concept of the patent, without knowledge of the invention, assume the mantle of the skilled but unimaginative person with common general knowledge at the priority date, identify the difference between the cited matter and the invention, then ask whether those differences constitute steps which would have been technically obvious or whether they require invention.

The test was restated by Jacob LJ in *Pozzoli SpA* v *BDMO SA* along the following lines:

1. (a) Identify the notional 'person skilled in the art'.

    (b) Identify the relevant common general knowledge of that person.

2. Identify the inventive concept of the claim in question or, if that cannot readily be done, construe it.

3. Identify what, if any, differences exist between the matter cited as forming part of the 'state of the art' and the inventive concept of the claim or the claim as construed.

4. Viewed without any knowledge of the alleged invention as claimed, do those differences constitute steps which would have been obvious to the person skilled in the art or do they require a degree of invention?

The inventive step must not have been obvious to a skilled person at the time of the invention as the next step to take; neither should it have been obvious to them to undertake trials to that end.

A member of the public would not be a useful comparator. Many people, especially with the advanced technologies, would find it all a mystery and would never understand how the invention worked or find it obvious, even if it were explained to them in great detail. The question of obviousness depends on the facts of each case. The existence of a long-felt want could indicate that the solution was not obvious. Large sales, however, may be due to other reasons, such as fashion, an effective marketing campaign or a better method of manufacture, rather than the inventiveness of this particular product or process. What matters is whether or not the innovation is technically obvious.

✎ EXAM TIP

It has been accepted that the *Windsurfing/Pozzoli* test is only to be regarded as guidance because it is not appropriate for as-yet undiscovered technologies. However, it is worth showing your examiner that you are aware that failure to apply these principles in court would probably result in an appeal.

KEY CASE

Conor Medsystems Inc. v *Angiotech Pharmaceuticals Inc.* [2008] RPC 28, HL

Concerning: what to consider when identifying whether an inventive step was obvious

Facts

A stent was coated with TAXOL to prevent damage to the heart muscles during the process of angioplasty. Many drugs including TAXOL (a cure for cancer) could be tested. The specification only indicated that TAXOL *might* work and did not explain *how* it worked. Conor, opposing registration, claimed that as any skilled person could say that something was worth trying (*might* work) the patent was not inventive.

Legal principle

There was no requirement that the specification had to explain how or why an invention worked. If there was enough in the specification to show that it was plausible that TAXOL would work, that was sufficient.

Industrial application

> **KEY STATUTE**
>
> ### Section 4 Patents Act 1977
>
> '. . . an invention shall be taken to be capable of industrial application if it can be made or used in any kind of industry, including agriculture.'

The most important issues related to industrial application will be dealt with under the heading of exclusions. Other than that, the description must disclose at least one way that the invention can be used (see Sharples, 2011). But remember, it does not have to be better, cheaper or quicker than what came before; it just needs to be different.

> **KEY CASE**
>
> ### *Human Genome Sciences Inc.* v *Eli Lilly & Co.* [2011] UKSC 51, SC
> *Concerning: what constitutes industrial application in relation to biotech inventions*
>
> #### Facts
> A patent claim to a nucleotide sequence of a gene lacked specific information about potential uses of the invention.
>
> #### Legal principle
> Where, in the light of the common general knowledge, a new substance has a plausible claimed use, this can satisfy the requirement of industrial application. This must be contrasted with the case where the patent application merely indicates that a programme of research should be undertaken to determine whether the substance has a particular effect.

This decision accords with jurisprudence at the European Patent Office (EPO) but this lower threshold requiring only that it be plausible must be treated with some caution. Due to policy reasons it may be limited to biotechnological inventions (see Sharples, 2012).

Exclusions

> **KEY STATUTE**
>
> ### Sections 1(2) Patents Act 1977
>
> '. . . the following (amongst other things) are not inventions for the purposes of this Act, that is to say, anything which consists of –
>
> (a) a discovery, scientific theory or mathematical method;
>
> (b) a literary, dramatic, musical or artistic work or any other aesthetic creation . . . ;

(c) a scheme, rule or method for performing a mental act, playing a game or doing business or a program for a computer;

(d) the presentation of information;

[but this] shall prevent anything from being treated as an invention . . . only to the extent that a patent or application for a patent relates to that thing *as such*.' (emphasis added)

Also excluded are patents which are regarded as contrary to public policy or morality, methods of treatment of the human or animal body by surgery or therapy, or of diagnosis practised on the human or animal body.

Some of the exclusions can be justified on the grounds of lack of technical effect. Many are abstract and related to information rather than inventions and more appropriately protected by copyright. Some are regarded as discoveries or knowledge that should be available for all to use, such as mathematical methods and the treatment or diagnosis of the human or animal body. However, treatment implies that there is some sort of illness or disease. Although such treatment is denied patent protection, it is perfectly acceptable to patent a drug which is used in the treatment. Some exclusions are more controversial, such as those relating to computer programs and business methods (see Chapter 11).

! Don't be tempted to . . .

Don't forget to bear in mind that the tests for industrial application under section 3 and patentability under section 1 are separate. It is also important to remember that many of the things which are not to be regarded as inventions are abstract or intellectual and are more suited to being protected by copyright. Some, however, are excluded for public policy reasons (see Pila, 2010). There is a feeling that methods of treatment should be available for all doctors or vets to use to treat their patients, even though the drugs used in those treatments may be granted a patent. A monopoly is regarded as necessary to make sure that the considerable research and development costs of pharmaceutical companies are recouped to enable them to continue with further research leading to further innovation.

✓ Make your answer stand out

Many patented inventions arise out of a discovery but something further, some technical effect, is needed to make that discovery patentable. Make your answer stand out by commenting that this is very important in areas such as genetic engineering. See Aerts (2004).

> ### ✎ EXAM TIP
>
> Showing that you are aware of the 'bigger picture' is likely to please your examiner. So explain that, even though the aim of both the EPO and UK Intellectual Property Office is for European harmonisation, they may have different views and that English courts, although decisions of other states have strong persuasive value, are subject to *stare decisis*. Different courts may apply the same principles but to a different standard (see Sharples, 2011). This creates not only lack of legal certainly but also higher costs and the potential for 'forum shopping'. These problems should be reduced, however, with the introduction of the Unified Patents Court. Keep in mind, when answering any question in this area, that exclusions are made for policy reasons and not because there is a coherent reason for them. Why should doctors be prevented from patenting their methods of treatment while drugs companies are able to monopolise life-saving drugs? Also offer practical advice, stressing that the first advice that should be given to any prospective patentee is to keep their invention confidential. If in doubt, say nowt!

■ Entitlement

The inventor is the actual deviser (or joint devisers) of the invention. The question is who is responsible for the inventive concept underlying the invention?

> ### KEY CASE
>
> *IDA Ltd* v *University of Southampton* [2006] RPC 21, ChD
> *Concerning: right to be considered the inventor*
>
> #### Facts
>
> A university professor invented a cockroach trap which caused poisoned electronically charged talcum powder to attach to the legs of the insects. Having read about the invention, Mr Metcalf, although not knowing that the powder became attached to the insects, correctly suggested to the professor that magnetic powder might be more efficient than an electrostatically charged powder. The professor applied for a new patent using magnetic powder. It was decided that Mr Metcalf was the inventor after a dispute arose as to who had the right to the patent.
>
> #### Legal principle
>
> To be considered as an inventor a person does not have to be skilled in the art in question: all that is required is that the person provided the inventive aspect to the patent. Having common general knowledge was not enough to be inventive. Routine trials are not inventive; the question is whether they had contributed the heart of the invention.

Anyone may apply for a patent but the inventor must be identified in the application. A patent will only be granted to someone who is entitled to it, the inventor, their employer or someone to whom the invention has been transferred. Under section 7(1) of the Patents Act 1977, a patent may be granted primarily to the inventor or joint inventors. However, this is subject to others being entitled by virtue of any enactment or rule of law, etc. or enforceable term in an agreement entered into with the inventor before the making of the invention. Section 39 is also relevant and provides that the inventor's employer will be entitled to the patent where it is made in the course of the employee's normal or specifically assigned duties, in circumstances where the invention might reasonably be expected to result from carrying out those duties. Another exception applies where an employee has a special obligation to further the interests of the employer's undertaking, for example, in the case of a managing director.

Ownership

Most inventions are uncontroversial as to ownership and are made in the course of employment by people employed to invent. Disputes arise either where there is no expectation of invention on the employee's part but the employment contract attempts to claim ownership of all an employee's intellectual output, or where the inventor is in a managerial position within the company. Directors owe fiduciary duties to their company. They must always put the company's interests before their own and will be held to be under a special obligation to work in the best interests of the company. There is, however, a grey area in relation to lower-level managers where it is uncertain whether they owe such a special obligation or not.

■ Employee compensation

Where an invention belonging to an employer has been made by an employee and the invention or the patent (or both) is of outstanding benefit to the employer, having regard, inter alia, to the size and nature of the employer's undertaking, the court or comptroller may award the employee compensation where it is just to do so (section 40). The first award was made to two research scientists who formulated a compound used in radioactive imaging subject to a patent owned by their employer in *Kelly* v *GE Healthcare* [2009] RPC 12. The awards were £1 million and £500,000 respectively (see Howell, 2011).

■ Putting it all together

Answer guidelines

See the essay question at the start of the chapter.

Approaching the question

When asked to explain, you need to write clearly and support what you say with relevant authority. However, in effect, you are then asked to criticise the definition provided. To do this you must examine the strengths and weaknesses of the definition, justifying your conclusions with authority.

Important points to include

- Start by considering what an invention is.
- Novelty and the state of the art should be discussed (*Synthon*).
- Describe the unimaginative but highly knowledgeable skilled person.
- Explain that the hypothetical presence of a skilled person in public is needed to destroy novelty (*Lux*).
- Now, inventive step. Explain the statutory test and that the *Windsurfing/Pozzoli* questions are just guidance.
- The difference between novelty and the obvious concerning previously filed but not yet published patents can be commented upon.
- Include the need for the invention to be capable of industrial application.
- It is now time to consider the exclusions.
- You must then consider whether the suggested definition is indeed a good one.
- You may conclude that it seems oversimplified. Explain that innovations that are not regarded as capable of industrial application are not alluded to in this definition. An innovation may be non-obvious and an advance but may still not receive patent protection.

✓ **Make your answer stand out**

Explain that there is no definition of an invention because such a definition could reduce flexibility and could become a fetter on the development of the law in line with technological developments.

- Discuss the policy reasons relating to the exclusions, showing your grasp of the 'bigger picture'.

- Discussing sufficiency demonstrates insight into the problems associated with inventing a way of making a product that was known to exist but could not previously be made.

READ TO IMPRESS

Aerts, R.J. (2004) 'The industrial applicability and utility requirements for the patenting of genomic inventions: a comparison between European and US law', 26(8) *EIPR*, 349.

Batteson, A. and Karet, I. (2009) '*Lundbeck* v *Generics* – "biogen insufficiency" explained', 31(1) *EIPR*, 51.

Howell, C. (2011) 'Extra compensation for inventive employees' 4 *IPQ*, 371

Pila, J. (2010) 'On the European requirement for an invention', 41(8) *International Review of Intellectual Property and Competition Law*, 906.

Sharples, A. (2011) 'Industrial applicability for genetic patents – divergence between the EPO and the UK', 33(2) *EIPR*, 72.

Sharples, A. (2012) 'Industrial applicability, patents and the Supreme Court' 34(4) *EIPR*, 284

Sharples, A. and Curley, D. (2006) 'Experimental novelty: *Synthon* v *SmithKline Beecham*', 28(5) *EIPR*, 308.

Smith, H. (2007) 'Patents: obviousness – *Windsurfing* test restated', 29(10) *EIPR*, N118.

www.pearsoned.co.uk/lawexpress

Go online to access more revision support including quizzes to test your knowledge, sample questions with answer guidelines, podcasts you can download, and more!

Patent infringement, defences and remedies

6

Revision checklist

Essential points you should know:

- [ ] What acts infringe a patent
- [ ] What knowledge is required of the infringer
- [ ] How the scope of the invention is determined
- [ ] The function of the reader skilled in the art
- [ ] What is meant by a variant having a material effect
- [ ] The time at which the reader skilled in the art should consider the claim
- [ ] The view the skilled reader should take about the language of the claim
- [ ] Defences to a patent infringement action
- [ ] Remedies for patent infringement
- [ ] What constitutes a groundless threats action

■ Topic map

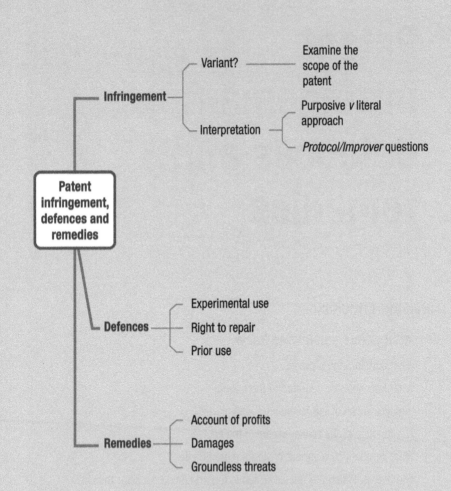

▇ Introduction

A patent proprietor has a right to prevent all third parties from making or using the patented product or process without their consent.

Infringement occurs if a patented product or process is exploited within the UK without the patentee's consent. The nature of infringing acts differs depending on whether the patent is for a product or for a process. Some forms of infringement relating to patented processes and supplying the means to put the patent into effect require a form of knowledge. However, knowledge is not required for other forms of infringement such as making, disposing of, importing, etc. a patented product.

It is common for a defendant in infringement proceedings to challenge the validity of the patent. If the patent is found to be invalid or partially invalid to a relevant extent, that will provide a complete defence and the claimant will have lost the patent forever.

Barring a claim of invalidity, if a patent is merely copied, infringement proceedings may be quite straightforward. Problems arise where the invention has not been taken in its entirety but some feature has been changed or an additional feature included. Before it can be decided whether a patent has been infringed the invention must be defined. This entails looking at what has been specified in the claim, using the description and drawings to determine the purpose in the context of the language used. The interpretation of the specification has caused debate within the European Patent Convention (EPC) countries and the EPO. In granting the strong monopoly right of a patent it is necessary to achieve a balance between fair protection of the patentee and a reasonable degree of certainty for third parties.

ASSESSMENT ADVICE

Essay questions

An essay question may ask you to explain the development from the literal to the purposive approach of the interpretation of a patent claim, including the status of the Protocol to Article 69 of the EPC. You will need to demonstrate an understanding not only of the relevant case law but also of the consequences to the patentee and third parties of each approach.

Problem questions

A problem question could include issues relating to validity, prior use, defences such as repair and experimental use, and remedies. Although you must make sure that you ▶

identify and deal with the main issues thoroughly, you must also ensure that any other points have been considered and dealt with in the depth appropriate for the question asked. Remember, it is how you apply your knowledge that will get you good marks. Make sure that your advice makes sense, is not conflicting and that the strengths and weaknesses of each issue are made clear.

■ Sample question

Could you answer this question? Below is a typical problem question that could arise on this topic. Guidelines on answering the question are included at the end of this chapter, whilst a sample essay question and guidance on tackling it can be found on the companion website.

PROBLEM QUESTION

Wendy invented and patented 'Dobbinsafe', an air-cooled horse exercise boot. The specification states that the boot is intended to prevent damage to a horse's leg caused by exercise-induced strain or by external striking. The boot is formed of a leg-embracing collar secured around a horse's leg and the surface of the boot includes at least one air intake, exit outlets and channels connecting the intake and outlets to allow coolant air or fluid to penetrate the surface and pass from one part of the boot to the other, hitting the horse's leg as it gallops. Wendy is aware that an Italian product, 'Ridesure', is being marketed in the UK. This horse exercise boot includes an outer layer which is made up of small holes throughout with an inner layer of foamed permeable material. This will allow air to flow into the boot and reach the leg when the horse is galloping. Wendy feels that the Ridesure boot infringes her patent.

Advise Wendy on the likelihood of an infringement action succeeding and what remedies are available if her patent is found to have been infringed.

■ Infringement

KEY DEFINITION: Patent infringement

Infringement of a UK patent occurs if a validly patented product or process is exploited within the UK without the patentee's consent in the absence of a valid defence.

Remember that if **patent infringement** proceedings are commenced it is common for the defendant to challenge the validity of the patent (this explains in part why patent infringement actions are so expensive). If successful, there will be no valid patent and therefore no infringement.

> ## ! Don't be tempted to . . .
>
> Don't let the facts worry you. The facts of cases in this area can seem very confusing to non-scientists but the law itself is on the whole quite clear. Although there has been a conflict between the interpretation of the English courts and those of some other European countries, this problem should be reduced in the future when the Unified Patent Court comes into existence.

KEY STATUTE

Section 60(1) and (2) Patents Act 1977

A person infringes a patent for an invention if in the UK and while the patent is in force they, without the consent of the proprietor, make, dispose of, offer to dispose of, use, import or keep a patented product. Where the invention is a process, a person infringes a patent if they use or offer it for use when they know, or it is obvious to a reasonable person in the circumstances, that its use in the UK without the consent of the proprietor would be an infringement of the patent. Infringement also occurs where, if the invention is a process, a person disposes of, offers to dispose of, uses, imports or keeps any product which was obtained directly by means of that process. In addition a person also infringes a patent if in the UK they supply or offer to supply any of the means, relating to an essential element of the invention, for putting the invention into effect when they know, or it is obvious to a reasonable person in the circumstances, that those means are suitable for putting, and are intended to put, the invention into effect in the UK.

✎ EXAM TIP

Be careful about considering the culpability of the infringer to determine whether damages are available. Do not forget that the knowledge required of the infringer is different depending on whether you are talking about a product or a process. There is no requirement of knowledge for infringement of a product under section 60(1); liability is strict unless there is a defence available. For infringement of a process it must be obvious to a reasonable person that the patent is being infringed. In addition, in section 60(2) the act of 'supplying the means' has been interpreted as meaning that if a supplier knows, or it is obvious to a reasonable person in the circumstances, that an ultimate user would adapt the non-infringing product in a way that will infringe, the supplier will be liable.

What if there is a variant?

If an invention has been copied exactly, the only problems that may arise will relate to the validity of the patent and any defences. However, if the alleged infringing product or process is a variant of the patented product or process, this may still give rise to a successful infringement action. It depends on the scope of the patent and whether the variant falls within it.

Examine the scope of the patent

Section 125(1) of the Patents Act 1977 is in effect the same as Article 69 of the EPC and states that the invention is regarded as what is specified in the claim as interpreted in the description and any drawings.

KEY STATUTE

Section 125(1) Patents Act 1977

'An invention for a patent for which an application has been made or for which a patent has been granted shall, unless the context otherwise requires, be taken to be that specified in a claim of the specification as interpreted by the description and any drawings contained in that specification. The extent of the protection conferred by a patent shall be determined accordingly.'

For comparison, Article 69(1) of the European Patent Convention states:

'The extent of the protection conferred by a European Patent . . . shall be determined by the claims. Nevertheless, the description and drawings shall be used to interpret the claims.'

Note that a number of provisions in the Patents Act 1977 are stated by section 130(7) to have been framed so as to have, as nearly as practicable, the same effects in the UK as the equivalent provisions in the EPC. For the purposes of this book, these include sections 1(1) to (4), 2 to 6, 60 and 125.

How is this to be interpreted?

The Protocol on the interpretation of Article 69 states that it should not be interpreted by the strict, literal meaning of the wording used in the claims, the description and drawings being employed only for the purpose of resolving any ambiguity. Neither should it be interpreted using the claims only as a guideline. A position between these extremes should be taken which combines a fair protection for the patentee with a reasonable degree of certainty for third parties.

> **!** **Don't be tempted to . . .**
>
> Don't confuse the interpretation of the claim with the interpretation of the Protocol. The Protocol concerns the interpretation of Article 69, not the interpretation of claims. Article 69 EPC states that the extent of the protection must be determined from the claims (using the description and drawings). We are still left with the question of how the courts should interpret the claim.

The purposive v literal approach

KEY DEFINITION: Purposive approach

The purposive approach looks at the purpose or reason for making the claim.

The literal approach is the traditional approach taken by lawyers in the UK. It provides great certainty to third parties. Any deviation from the words in the claim will mean there is no infringement. For example, if a product having three appendages is claimed, one having four such appendages would escape an infringement action. This explains why patent agents tended to use words in claims such as 'plurality' rather than expressing a precise number.

The **purposive approach** looks at the purpose or reason for making the claim. Deviation from the words used can be quite wide but still fall within what may have been envisaged as intended to be claimed by the patentee. Making a minor but ineffectual variation in an attempt to escape the exact language of a claim would still infringe. This gives wider protection to the patentee but brings some uncertainty to third parties who may or may not find themselves having infringed the patent. It makes it more difficult to determine the boundaries of the claim.

KEY CASE

Catnic Components Ltd v *Hill & Smith Ltd* [1982] RPC 183, HL

Concerning: the interpretation of the claim and whether a minor variation would avoid a successful infringement action

Facts

The claimant had a patent for a lintel which stated that the rear face was vertical. The defendant was held to have infringed the patent, having made a similar lintel but with a rear face which was slightly inclined from the vertical.

Legal principle

A patent specification should be given a purposive construction aimed at the skilled worker in the field rather than the pure literal interpretation favoured by lawyers.

In order to take a balanced approach, one must ask whether a **person skilled in the art** would understand that strict compliance with a particular word or phrase was intended by the patentee to be an essential requirement of the invention. If so, any variant that did not comply with that word or phrase would fall outside the claim regardless of whether it had any effect. If the variant did have a material effect, there would be no infringement.

KEY DEFINITION: Person skilled in the art

The person skilled in the art is an unimaginative person, or team of uninventive people, with the common general knowledge available to a person in the relevant field at the date of filing. They will only think the obvious and will not question general assumptions.

✎ EXAM TIP

Show that you are aware that a purposive interpretation can lead to greater protection for the patentee but uncertainty for the third party who, having read the specification, may infringe unintentionally. Although a fair balance is needed, you could observe that the patentee has the opportunity to draft their claim as widely as they choose and if they fail to do so they have only themselves to blame. But there is a danger in drafting a claim widely as this might cover prior art and invalidate the claim for want of novelty.

The *Protocol* questions (formally known as the *Improver* questions)

The *Catnic* case demonstrated that, in using the purposive interpretation, 'vertical' would easily be seen by the skilled person as being intended to include 'slightly off vertical'. There was a greater problem of interpretation, for example, if the variant was a rubber rod with slits in it when the patented product claimed a helical spring. Both the patented product and the variant were used to remove hair from ladies' legs.

KEY CASE

Improver Corp. v *Raymond Industries Ltd* **[1991] FSR 223, CA (Hong Kong)**
Concerning: guidance on how to interpret a claim when there is an equivalent

Facts

(At the time of this case, the UK Patents Act 1977 was in force in Hong Kong.)

The claimant had a patent for the 'Epilady', a device claiming use of a helical spring for removing hair from arms and legs. The defendant had a similar device called 'Smooth & Silky' which performed the same function but used a rubber rod with slits in it rather than a spring. This was held to be outside the claim.

Legal principle

The court should ask itself the following three questions:

1. Does the variant have a material effect on the way the invention works? If yes, the variant is outside the claim (and does not infringe). If no?

2. Would this (i.e. that the variant had no material effect) have been obvious at the date of publication of the patent to a reader skilled in the art? If no, the variant is outside the claim. If yes?

3. Would the reader skilled in the art nevertheless have understood from the language of the claim that the patentee intended that strict compliance with the primary meaning was an essential requirement of the invention? If yes, the variant is outside the claim.

Note: The court followed *Catnic* and the reformulation of the *Catnic* questions set out by Hoffmann J in *Improver Corp.* v *Remington Consumer Products Ltd*, involving the same devices.

We are left with having to decide what a person skilled in the art would have understood the patentee to have used the language of the claim to mean. Remember, however, that the *Protocol/Improver* questions merely provide guidance in trying to address this problem (see *Kirin-Amgen*, below). The courts do not intend to give the patentee more than can be found within the claim.

! Don't be tempted to . . .

Don't forget about *new* areas of high technology. The *Protocol/Improver* questions may not be helpful in a rapidly developing high technology field such as genetic engineering. Whether a patentee should have worded their claim to include a rubber rod in addition to a spring may be an obvious and reasonable expectation. A patentee in a rapidly developing field would have to word their claim in a way that included the new, as yet unheard-of, technology (see *Kirin-Amgen*). Surely an impossibility!

KEY CASE

Kirin-Amgen Inc. v *Hoechst Marion Roussel Ltd* [2005] RPC 9, HL

Concerning: whether the Protocol *questions could be used to decide whether the skilled person could envisage how a new technology would work*

Facts

The claimants, KA, were the proprietors of a patent which used DNA technology in a host cell to artificially produce a hormone, EPO. This increased the production of red ▶

blood cells in the kidney, thereby increasing iron uptake. It was found that the defendant had not infringed this patent by making EPO using a variant of the process. It would not in this case have been obvious to a person skilled in the art that the variant worked in the same way as the invention, nor would they regard the claim as being sufficiently general to be intending to cover unknown technology at the time the claim was drafted.

Legal principle

The *Protocol* questions are merely a guide to determine what the person skilled in the art would have understood the patentee to be using the language of the claim to mean. It is the principle laid down in *Catnic* that must be followed.

✎ EXAM TIP

Highlight that despite the purposive approach it is still up to the inventor to specify the extent of their monopoly. If they have not claimed something it is not up to the court to rewrite the specification. They may have left something out for a sensible reason, such as avoiding prior art or the accusation of lack of inventive step. Remind your reader that the patents and their claims are meant to be statements made by the patentee to the relevant public, and their meaning and effect should be clear from reading the document.

When asking the second *Protocol/Improver* question it is easy to see that it should have been obvious that a helical spiral could have the same effect as a rubber rod with slits. It is far less easy to see how a patentee could have intended to cover something in their claim that had not yet been invented at the filing date. It could not have been obvious to the skilled person as they had no concept of its existence and so the second *Improver* question is not appropriate in this sort of circumstance. It is necessary, as stated in *Kirin-Amgen*, to fall back on *Catnic* and ask what the person skilled in the art would have understood the patentee to be using the language of the claim to mean. If that language can be construed to cover things not yet in existence, then there can be infringement; if not, there will be no infringement.

✓ Make your answer stand out

The article by Curley and Sheraton (2005) clearly follows the development of the interpretation of Article 69, discussing the *Catnic, Improver* and *Kirin-Amgen* cases. Make your answer stand out by explaining that they argue that in *Amgen* Lord Hoffmann concludes that the *Catnic* approach to construction which led to the *Protocol/Improver* questions was 'precisely in accordance with the protocol' but that the *Improver* questions are merely guidelines useful in interpreting the law.

Lord Hoffmann, the authors state, also makes it plain that, although it is not possible to extend the scope of the patent, it is acceptable to take due account of any element which is equivalent to an element specified in the claims. This would be an important part of the background of facts known to the skilled person which would affect what they understood the claim to mean. The late Professor Laddie, however, argued that *Kirin-Amgen* was wrongly decided and that there should be an extension of protection beyond the claim in line with the German interpretation of the Protocol. See Laddie (2009).

Defences

You must always pause to consider whether a defence is available, even if you quickly discount the possibility. The exceptions to infringement are set out in section 60(5)(a) to (i). They include acts done for private and non-commercial uses, experimental purposes, the extemporaneous making-up in a pharmacy of a medicine for an individual. Defences also include when an invention has been worked, or serious preparations to work it have been made before the priority date, or where ships, aircraft, etc. are for a limited time (even if frequently) or accidentally in the UK. There are also defences aimed at farmers: an unlikely topic for an examination question, and where there is exhaustion of rights under European Union law. It must always be kept in mind that if an infringement action is started the defendant may in return attack the validity of the patent, most commonly attempting to have it revoked for lack of novelty or inventive step.

Experimental use

There are some things that are no threat to the commercial exploitation of the patent and may indeed benefit the furtherance of knowledge in our society. These things are therefore specifically allowed.

KEY STATUTE

Section 60(5) Patents Act 1977

'An act which, apart from this subsection, would constitute an infringement of a patent for an invention shall not do so if –

(a) It is done privately and for purposes which are non-commercial

(b) It is done for experimental purposes relating to the subject-matter of the invention . . .'

There is a defence of private use but the use must be for the person's own use *and* not for any commercial purposes. If there were mixed purposes, one to generate information and one to make a profit, you must establish which was the main purpose.

KEY CASE

Auchincloss v *Agricultural & Veterinary Supplies Ltd* **[1997] RPC 649, CA**

Concerning: what acts amounted to experimental use for section 60(5)(b)

Facts

The patent was for a dry, water-soluble biocidal composition which the claimant alleged had been infringed by the manufacture of an experimental sample which had been made for and supplied to MAFF by the defendant in order to obtain official approval.

Legal principle

Trials to discover something unknown or to test a hypothesis are regarded as legitimate experiments, but trials carried out to reaffirm what is already known or to show that a product works or to obtain official approval are not.

In addition, a monopoly should not be allowed to inhibit scientific developments, and as experimental use does not pose a threat to the patent holder it is allowed. Experimentation must be on the invention itself; it cannot be use of the invention for experimental purposes on something else.

✎ EXAM TIP

Experimentation is often illegitimately undertaken during the life of a patent in order to enter the market swiftly as soon as the patent expires. It would make your answer stand out if you included some mention of available remedies such as post-expiry injunctions or 'springboard relief'. The courts have granted injunctions to run after the expiry of the patent in order to prevent a person selling articles made during the subsistence of the patent, thus putting them in the position they would have been in if they had not 'jumped the gun'. However, point out that such relief is unlikely and damages may be a more appropriate remedy.

Right to repair

KEY STATUTE

Section 60(1)(a) Patents Act 1977

A person infringes a patent for a product invention if they *make* the product.

We can see that there may be a fine line between making a product, which is an infringement, and repairing a product, which is allowed. To repair something is not to make it. However, making and repairing are mutually exclusive, and which it is a question of fact.

KEY CASE

Schutz (UK) Ltd v *Werit UK Ltd* [2013] UKSC 16

Concerning: the existence and scope of the right of repair

Facts

The claimant was the exclusive licensee of a patent for an intermediate bulk container, a large metal cage into which a large plastic bottle was fitted used for transporting liquids. The cage was long-lasting but the bottles often needed to be replaced. The defendant supplied replacement bottles and claimed that they were repairing, not making the patented product.

Legal principle

'Makes' has no precise meaning; it is a matter of fact and degree and depends on the circumstances. One must consider whether the part being replaced was a subsidiary rather than a main component of the article, whether there was a much shorter life expectancy, whether it was free-standing and replaceable and whether, as here, there was no connection with the claimed inventive concept. On these facts the defendant was repairing, not making the article.

We can see here that there is a need to protect the patentee's monopoly whilst not stifling reasonable competition.

Prior use

KEY STATUTE

Section 64(1) Patents Act 1977

'Where a patent is granted for an invention, a person who in the United Kingdom before the priority date of the invention –

(a) does in good faith an act which would constitute an infringement of the patent if it were in force, or

(b) makes in good faith effective and serious preparations to do such an act,

has the right to continue to do the act or, as the case may be, to do the act, notwithstanding the grant of the patent; but this right does not extend to granting a licence to another person to do the act.'

This defence will only be available where the prior use was in good faith. It would typically be secret use (such as not to make it available to the public); otherwise it would destroy the novelty of the patent. Section 64, however, only provides a defence and there is no right to license others to do the prior act. Although sometimes described as a defence, it provides the prior user a right to continue the use or commence the use, where appropriate.

✓ **Make your answer stand out**

Make your answer stand out by explaining that patent protection aims to balance the benefit to society by encouraging innovation and the spread of knowledge with the monopoly given to the patentee. Section 64 is part of that balance and is intended to safeguard the existing commercial activity of a person in the UK which may have been overtaken by the subsequent grant of a patent. It is not, however, meant to allow them to expand into other areas at the expense of the patentee. Hence, although it depends on the circumstances, 'effective' must be more than just preparation to do an act; the infringing act must be about to be done. For a clear explanation of section 64 and why the problem might arise see Cohen and Davies (1994).

Remedies

The remedies available for infringement of a patent are found in section 61 and include an injunction, a discretionary remedy, an order for delivery up or destruction, damages, an account of profits, and a declaration that the patent is valid and has been infringed by the defendant.

✎ **EXAM TIP**

When discussing these remedies it would be worth explaining that they are a non-exhaustive list and could be expanded. Do not forget that damages and an account of profits are alternatives and may not, by section 61(2), both be awarded in respect of the same infringement. So do not ask for a remedy that is not available. However, do not omit to mention that the court has discretion to award damages in lieu of, or in addition to, an injunction. Also remember the impact of the Intellectual Property (Enforcement, etc.) Regulations 2006/1028 and the Directive on the enforcement of intellectual property rights (discussed in Chapter 3).

Account of profits

Bear in mind that the purpose of an account of profits is not to punish the defendant but to prevent their unjust enrichment. They are an alternative to damages but are rarely asked for in patent cases because of the complexity in quantifying them.

Damages

Damages are often based on the value of the royalties that the infringer would have paid had they taken a licence. Otherwise damages will be based on normal considerations of causation and remoteness, but you would not normally be expected to discuss these issues in any depth unless you are specifically asked to do so. A difficult issue in patent cases in particular is whether parasitic damages are available. These typically relate to the sale of non-infringing products made on the back of the sale of infringing products.

Groundless threats of infringement proceedings

There is a remedy of groundless threats of infringement proceedings under section 70. This allows a person aggrieved to bring an action against any person threatening proceedings, whether the patent proprietor or someone else. The person bringing the threats action is entitled to a declaration that the threats are unjustified, an injunction and damages for loss resulting from the threats. An example is where a threat is made against a distributor or retailer of a product alleged to infringe a patent. A person aggrieved in such a situation may be the distributer or retailer, or it could be the maker of the product who has lost outlets for their products as a result of the threats.

If the defendant shows that the acts in question infringe, or would infringe, the patent, the claimant must show that the patent is invalid in a material respect, and, even then, the defendant escapes if they can show that at the time the threats were made they did not know and had no reasonable grounds for knowing that the patent was invalid in that respect. Certain types of threats do not come within the action, such as threats relating to the making or importing for disposal of a product or using a process, or where the threat is made to the person actually making or importing for disposal the product or using the process (in respect of doing anything else in relation to the product or process).

Furthermore, it is not a threat to provide factual information about the patent or to make enquiries for the sole purpose of discovering by whom the patent has been infringed by making or importing the product for disposal or using the process, or making an assertion for the purpose of any enquiries so made.

It is also a defence if the person making the threats has used their best endeavours to identify the relevant person (for example, the person making the product) and they inform the person threatened of this before or at the time of making the threats, setting out the endeavours used.

✎ EXAM TIP

Groundless threats may be part of a problem question on infringement. Be aware that great care must be taken by the person making the threat to ensure they do not trigger a groundless threats action. Careless drafting of a threats letter could leave a patent proprietor exposed to being required to prove that the acts complained of infringe the patent and also leave the patent vulnerable to a challenge to its validity. In this way, groundless threats actions can be seen as a case of 'put up or shut up'.

Be aware that groundless threats actions are also available in relation to design rights and trade marks.

■ Putting it all together

Answer guidelines

See the problem question at the start of the chapter.

Approaching the question

Problem questions are intended to test your ability in applying legal principles to complex factual situations. Do not summarise the facts of the scenario but go to the heart of the problem by identifying the relevant legal issues.

Important points to include

- To decide whether there has been infringement you must first determine what is the monopoly claimed by Wendy.
- Section 125 says you must look at the claim, description and any drawings. Here the claim is for the 'air intake, exit outlets and channels connecting the intake and

outlets to allow coolant air or fluid to penetrate the surface, pass from one part of the boot to the other, hitting the horse's leg as it gallops'.

- In *Catnic* it was stated that the purposive construction should be taken.

- Guidance is given on this approach in the three *Protocol/Improver* questions.

- In *Kirin-Amgen* it was stated that the question should be what the skilled person in the art would have understood the patentee to be using the language of the claim to mean.

- You could assume that the skilled person is knowledgeable in the field of exercise boots for horses.

- The question to be posed here is: Would the person skilled in the exercise boots field understand that in Wendy's boot the air or fluid was to be guided to the horse's leg through the outlets and channels alone, or would they understand that she was claiming that the air was to flow freely throughout any permeable material?

- If you decide on the former there is no infringement, and if on the latter there could be infringement if there are no defences.

- When discussing remedies, you should mention that an injunction is the most common remedy sought and that although an account of profits is available it is an alternative to damages.

✓ **Make your answer stand out**

Stress that you understand that taking the literal approach to the interpretation of the claim would mean that any derivation from the words of the claim will not give rise to infringement, while adopting the purposive approach would give Wendy much stronger protection. You could also point out that although the *Protocol/Improver* questions are only guidance, failing to ask these questions may give rise to an appeal.

READ TO IMPRESS

Cohen, S. and Davies, I. (1994) 'Section 64 of the UK Patents Act 1977: right to continue use begun before priority date', 16(6) *EIPR*, 239.

Curley, D. and Sheraton, H. (2005) 'The Lords rule in *Amgen* v *TKT*', 27(4) *EIPR*, 154.

Freeland, R. and Blachman, G. (2009) 'The law of insufficiency: is *Biogen* still good law?', 31(9) *EIPR*, 478.

Laddie, H. (2009) '*Kirin-Amgen* – the end of equivalents in England?' 40(1) *International Review of Intellectual Property and Competition Law*, 31.

Moss, G. (2011) '*Virgin Atlantic* v *Contour & Delta Airlines* – patent actions brought back down to earth?', 33(11) *EIPR*, 699.

www.pearsoned.co.uk/lawexpress

Go online to access more revision support including quizzes to test your knowledge, sample questions with answer guidelines, podcasts you can download, and more!

Design law

7

Revision checklist

Essential points you should know:

- [ ] The rules for subsistence of the Community design and the UK registered design
- [ ] Definitions of 'design', 'product' and 'complex product'
- [ ] What 'novelty' and 'individual character' mean
- [ ] Key concepts such as 'informed user', 'design freedom', 'immaterial differences' and 'commonplace'
- [ ] The requirements for subsistence of the UK unregistered design right
- [ ] The meaning and scope of 'must-fit' and 'must-match'
- [ ] The similarities and differences between the various rights in designs
- [ ] What constitutes infringement of registered designs and unregistered designs

■ Topic map

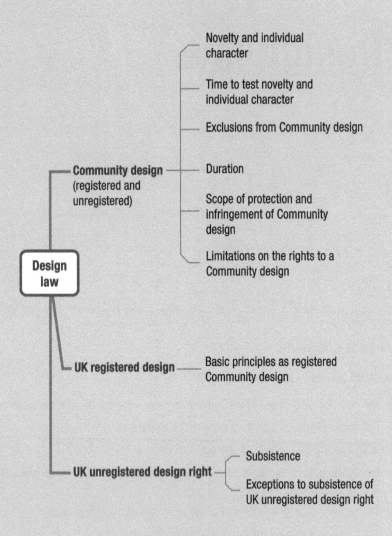

Design law

Community design (registered and unregistered)
— Novelty and individual character
— Time to test novelty and individual character
— Exclusions from Community design
— Duration
— Scope of protection and infringement of Community design
— Limitations on the rights to a Community design

UK registered design — Basic principles as registered Community design

UK unregistered design right
— Subsistence
— Exceptions to subsistence of UK unregistered design right

A printable version of this topic map is available from **www.pearsoned.co.uk/lawexpress**

■ Introduction

A design may be protected in a number of ways, especially by the Community design, the UK registered design and the UK design right.

Design law often appears complex to students because there are four main different forms of design right protection, being the Community design (registered and unregistered, RCD and UCD respectively), UK registered design (UKRD) and the UK unregistered design right (UDR). The latter is quite different from the other forms of protection for which the basic rules for registrability (for the RCD and UKRD) or subsistence (UCD) are basically the same. To make matters worse, there may also be some overlap with trade mark law and copyright. For example, a non-trivial and distinctive computer icon may be registered as a design (RCD and UKRD), protected by the UCD, registered as a trade mark and protected by copyright. It will not, however, be protected by the UDR.

ASSESSMENT ADVICE

Essay questions

You may be asked to discuss the protection of spare parts under design law, in particular under-the-bonnet parts and parts that have to be a particular shape to restore the original appearance of a complex article. Other areas ripe for essay questions include the rationale for two forms of Community design (registered and unregistered).

Problem questions

Problem questions on Community designs are likely to focus on registrability (RCD) or subsistence (UCD), exceptions and infringement. You may be asked to apply concepts such as the 'informed user', 'overall impression' and 'design freedom' to particular cases. For the UK unregistered design right, the effect of the permitted act under section 51 of the Copyright, Designs and Patents Act 1988, effectively suppresses copyright protection in design documents and models.

■ Sample question

Could you answer this question? Below is a typical essay question that could arise on this topic. Guidelines on answering the question are included at the end of this chapter, whilst a sample problem question and guidance on tackling it can be found on the companion website.

The existence of the UK's unregistered design right compromises the scheme of protection set out in the Community Design Regulation.

Critically discuss this statement with reference to subsistence of the rights and limitations to them.

📖 **REVISION NOTE**

Try thinking of a number of different products or articles and consider which of the design rights might apply to them, assuming that they are new and distinctive.

■ Community design

There are two forms of **Community design**, one subject to registration (RCD), the other informal (UCD). The basic requirements for both are the same (apart from the date at which novelty and individual character is tested).

KEY DEFINITION: Community design

A Community design has a unitary character and has equal effect throughout the Community. It may only be registered, transferred, surrendered, declared invalid or its use prohibited in relation to the entire Community (now EU).

The design must conform to the key definitions of 'design', 'product' or 'complex product'; it must be new and have individual character (and not fall within the exclusions; see later).

KEY STATUTE

Article 3 Community Design Regulation

'For the purposes of this Regulation:

"design" means the appearance of the whole or a part of a product resulting from the features of, in particular, the lines, contours, colours, shape, texture and/or materials of the product itself and/or its ornamentation;

"product" means any industrial or handicraft item, including *inter alia* parts intended to be assembled into a complex product, packaging, get-up, graphic symbols and typographic typefaces, but excluding computer programs;

"complex product" means a product which is composed of multiple components which can be replaced, permitting disassembly and re-assembly of the product.'

Article 4(1) Community Design Regulation
'A design shall be protected by a Community design to the extent that it is new and has individual character.'

Novelty and individual character

A design is new if no identical design (including a design with features which differ only in immaterial details) has been made available to the public. However, there is a proviso to this and a pre-existing design will be disregarded if it could not reasonably have become known in the normal course of business to the circles specialised in the sector concerned operating in the Community (now EU).

A design has an **individual character** if the overall impression it produces on an **informed user** differs from the overall impression produced on such a user by any design which has been made available to the public.

KEY CASE

Green Lane Products Ltd v PMS International Group Ltd **[2008] FSR 1, CA**
Concerning: Novelty and the scope of the prior art

Facts

A challenge to the validity of the claimant's Community design for spiky laundry balls was based on the defendant's similar-shaped spiky balls used for massaging the human body.

Legal principle

The prior art is not limited to the particular product for which the design was registered, as the scope of infringement is not limited to the product for which it was intended to apply the design. For example, the registration of a design applied to motor cars would protect also against its use for toys.

The purpose of the proviso about a design not being known in the normal course of business to the circles specialised in the sector concerned operating in the Community (EU) is to prevent counterfeiters outside Europe claiming some obscure prior art so as to defeat a Community design.

The 'informed user' is not the same as the 'average consumer' of trade mark law. The informed user has experience of similar products and will be reasonably discriminatory and able to appreciate sufficient detail to decide whether or not the design under consideration creates a different overall impression. The degree of design freedom is taken into account.

KEY CASE

Case C-281/10 P *PepsiCo Inc.* v *GrupoPromer Mon Graphic SA* [2011] ECR I-10153, CJEU

Concerning: The informed user

Facts

This design in question was for a promotional article having a disc shape with circular indentations and a raised edge, sometimes referred to as a 'pog', 'rapper' or 'tazo'. The design had been registered as a Community design but, following a challenge on the basis of an earlier registered design applied to circular metal plates for games, the design was declared invalid. The Board or appeal annulled that decision but was itself overruled by the General Court of the EU. The Court of Justice of the EU confirmed that the registration was invalid, confirming that the differences between the design and the earlier design were insufficient to produce an overall impression on the informed user that differed from that produced by the earlier design. In doing so, the Court of Justice gave guidance on the informed user.

Legal principle

1. The informed user is particularly observant because of his personal experience or extensive knowledge of the sector in question.

2. As the General Court observed, the informed user in the present case could be a child aged between five and ten years or a marketing manager whose company promotes its goods using 'pogs', 'rappers' or 'tazos'.

3. The informed user is not an expert or specialist capable of observing in detail minimal differences between the designs in conflict.

4. The informed user knows of various designs which exist in the sector, possesses a certain degree of knowledge of the features those design normally include and, as a result of his interest in the products in question, shows a relatively high degree of attention when he uses them.

5. Normally, the informed user will make a direct comparison between the conflicting designs. However, there may be times when this is impracticable or uncommon in the sector concerned. There is nothing in the Regulation to rule out an indirect comparison in appropriate circumstances.

Time to test novelty and individual character

The time when a design has been made available to the public differs between the RCD and the UCD. This is further complicated as the RCD provides for the priority of earlier applications elsewhere for up to six months.

- RCD relevant date is the date of filing the application, or earlier priority date if there is one.
- UCD relevant date is the date the design itself is first made available to the public.

There is a 12-month period of grace for the RCD so, for example, the designer may market products to the design during that period before filing the application to register.

'Under-the-bonnet' parts which are not seen during normal use of a complex product are not considered to be novel or to have individual character.

! Don't be tempted to . . .

Don't skip over the rules for the dates for testing novelty and individual character. Be aware of the impact of the period of grace and, if applicable, the priority date. These rules can often be very important in problem questions and a mistake can really mess up the rest of your answer. The figure below shows three possibilities (there are more).

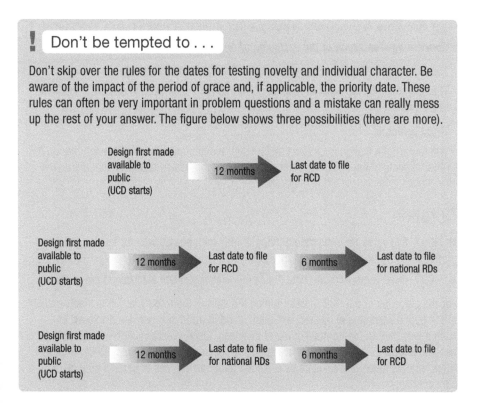

Exclusions from Community design

- Features dictated by technical function.
- 'Must-fit' features (except in respect of modular systems which are protectable in principle).
- Designs contrary to public policy or morality.
- 'Must-match' spare parts used to restore the original appearance of a complex product.

The last exception is easily missed as it is buried away in Article 110 of the Community Design Regulation (transitional provisions). The exception is subject to review but is likely to remain. Note that the presence of excepted features does not prevent protection of other features. For example, a design of a teapot with an overall shape which is well-known but which has a new design of spout having individual character may be protected. The scope of protection will be limited accordingly.

KEY CASE

***3M Innovative Properties Co.'s designs* (No. ICD000000040, 14 June 2004) OHIM**
Concerning: The scope of the exclusion of features dictated by function

Facts

The design in question was in respect of a swab on a stick used to dispense antiseptic to the skin.

Legal principle

Where part of a design is dictated by function, the informed user will concentrate on the other aspects of the design to determine whether the design has individual character.

Duration

- RCD – five years from the date of filing. It may then be renewed for further periods of five years up to a maximum of 25 years.
- UCD – three years from the date the design was first made available to the public.

For the purposes of the UCD in determining the start of the three years, it is made available to the public when it is published, exhibited, used in trade or otherwise disclosed in such a way that, in the normal course of business, these events could reasonably have become known to the circles specialised in the sector concerned within the Community. No account is taken of disclosure by a person under an express or implied duty of confidentiality.

! Don't be tempted to . . .

Don't assume that, being an informal right, the UCD is the same as a short-term copyright. The rules on subsistence, exceptions and infringement are different (though the same design may be protected by both rights, for example, in the case of an artistic work). Another important distinction is that the duration of the UCD is not measured from the end of the calendar year during which the design was created, but is based on the date that the design was first made available to the public.

Scope of protection and infringement of Community design

The scope of protection for a Community design resembles the test for individual character in that it is a question of whether the alleged infringing design, from the perspective of the informed user, does not produce a different overall impression compared with the protected design. Design freedom is taken into consideration.

KEY STATUTE

Article 10 Community Design Regulation

1. 'The scope of protection conferred by a Community design shall include any design which does not produce on the informed user a different overall impression.

2. In assessing the scope of protection, the degree of freedom of the designer in developing his design shall be taken into consideration.'

The registered Community design gives the right-holder a monopoly right which is infringed by a person using it without the right-holder's consent. Use, in particular, includes making, offering, putting on the market, importing, exporting or using a product in which the design is incorporated or applied, or stocking such a product for those purposes.

KEY CASE

Samsung Electronics (UK) Ltd v Apple Inc. **[2012] EWCA Civ 1430**
Concerning: Individual character

Facts

Samsung sought a declaration of non-infringement of Apple's Community registered design for a tablet computer.

Legal principle

It was important to understand that to infringe a registered Community design that there was no issue of copying (unless deferred publication applied). But it was essential to compare the alleged infringing products with the design registration and not with the actual iPads themselves, which bore little resemblance to the representations in the registration. The trial judge (who famously described Samsung's tablets as being not as cool as the iPad) was correct in holding that the differences between the Samsung tablets and the Apple registration would be such as to produce a different overall impression.

For the unregistered Community design, it is required that the use in question results from copying the protected design. This also applies during the period of deferred publication where the design is registered but publication has been deferred. An applicant to register a Community design can defer publication by up to 30 months from the filing date, hence delaying the payment of the publication fee.

KEY CASE

Procter & Gamble Co. v *Reckitt Benckiser (UK) Ltd* **[2008] FSR 8, CA**
Concerning: Individual character

Facts

This was a case on the alleged infringement of a registered Community design applied to a spray container for air fresheners.

Legal principle

To escape infringement, a design did not have to be 'clearly different' and it was sufficient if it differed in a way that the informed user was able to discriminate. The notional informed user would be fairly familiar with design issues and was more discriminating and careful than the average consumer of trade mark law. What mattered was what stuck in the mind of the informed user when he viewed the products, not after he had viewed them, and consequently, 'imperfect recollection' had a limited role to play. Where design freedom was limited, smaller differences could create a different overall impression. The trial judge erred by applying a 'stick in the mind' test rather than a 'what would impress now' test and his finding that there was infringement was reversed.

Limitations on the rights to a Community design

The rights to a Community design (registered or unregistered) do not extend to the following acts:

- Acts done privately and for non-commercial purposes.
- Acts done for experimental purposes.
- Reproduction for citation or teaching in accordance with fair practices without unduly prejudicing the normal exploitation of the design, providing the source is mentioned.
- Acts in respect of the repair of ships or aircraft temporarily in the Community.

Furthermore, the doctrine of exhaustion of rights applies to Community design. For the registered Community design, there are also provisions in relation to prior use commenced in good faith before the filing date (or priority date, if there is one), or, where serious and effective preparations have been made to commence use, providing such use did not involve copying the registered design.

✓ **Make your answer stand out**

Show that you understand the logical justification of having a registered and unregistered Community design as well as a period of grace. For example, it may be that the design in question has short-term commercial viability or the owner may wish to delay registration to see whether the design is a commercial success. In an essay question, use examples of designs applied to different types of products to bring your answer to life.

■ UK registered design

The UK registered design was modified substantially as a result of the Directive harmonising registered design law throughout the Community. As a result, the basic principles, such as subsistence and the scope of the rights of the owner, are virtually identical to those for the registered Community design except, of course, references to the Community are to the UK.

KEY CASE

Dyson Ltd v *Vax Ltd* [2010] FSR 39, ChD
Concerning: designs dictated by function

Facts

This involved the design of the transparent bin used for Dyson vacuum cleaners. Note, in the Court of Appeal ([2012] FSR 4), the issue was concerned with the application of the informed user test – see now the *PepsiCo* v *GruperPromer* case above which post-dated the Court of Appeal judgment.

Legal principle

The exception applies only in respect of designs dictated *solely* by function. The exception is not limited to cases where that and no other design could perform the function in question. Protection was denied to those features of a product's appearance that had been chosen exclusively for the purpose of designing a product that performed its function, as opposed to features that had been chosen at least to some degree for the purpose of enhancing a product's visual appearance. In the present case, the transparent bin was chosen for functional and aesthetic reasons.

✎ EXAM TIP

Be prepared to use authorities on the UK registered design in problems on the Community design and vice versa where issues of subsistence are involved as the basic rules are equivalent. Say why you are doing this and give appropriate weight to cases before the Court of Justice of the European Union.

The UK Registered Designs Act 1949, as amended, has specific provisions as to ownership and remedies (more detailed than is the case under the Community Design Regulation). For example, where the creation of a UK design occurs under a commission for money or money's worth, the person commissioning its creation will be entitled to be the proprietor of the design. The remedies for infringing a UK registered design are the same as for infringement of a Community design. There are also provisions for delivery up, disposal of infringing articles, etc.

KEY STATUTE

Section 24A(2) Registered Designs Act 1949; regulation 1A(2) Community Designs Regulations 2005/2339, as amended

In an action for infringement [of a Community design] all such relief by way of damages, injunctions, accounts or otherwise is available to him [to the holder of a Community design] as is available in respect of the infringement of any other property right.

Note: wording in brackets relevant to the Community design.

There is also a remedy for groundless threats of infringement proceedings which also applies in respect of a Community design (registered and unregistered). There is an equivalent remedy for the UK unregistered design right. As with other intellectual property rights, note should be taken of the provisions of the Directive on the enforcement of intellectual property rights, in particular Article 12 in relation to the assessment of damages.

! Don't be tempted to . . .

Don't think that the rules for determining ownership of (entitlement to) a Community design are the same as for the UK registered and unregistered design rights. In particular, there is no provision for the RCD or UCD to automatically vest in the commissioner of a design. A person commissioning the creation of a design protected under the Community Design Regulation must seek an assignment of the rights under the Regulation, as confirmed by the Court of Justice.

KEY CASE

Case C-32/08 *Fundación Española para la Innovación de la Artesanía (FEIA)* v *Cul de Sac EspacioCreativo SL* **[2009] ECR I-5611, CJEU**

Concerning: entitlement to design created under a commission

Facts

The claimant commissioned the defendant to create a new design for a cuckoo clock.

Legal principle

The terms 'employee' and 'employer' in the Community Design Regulation were not to be interpreted widely so as to include persons creating a design under a commission, even though such persons were paid contractually and under the direction of the commissioner. This must be contrasted with the entitlement to a UK registered design and the UK unregistered design right, both of which have specific provision for a person commissioning the creation of a design for money or money's worth to be the first proprietor or owner of the design.

UK unregistered design right

The UK unregistered design right was introduced by the Copyright, Designs and Patents Act 1988 in an attempt to overcome the problems of protection of functional designs by means of copyright in drawings showing the designs, as highlighted in *British Leyland Motor Corp v Armstrong Patents Co Ltd* [1986] 2 WLR 400.

✎ EXAM TIP

In problem questions on registered designs, always be prepared to consider whether there is unregistered design protection (whether the UK unregistered design right or unregistered Community design). Although the UK unregistered design right is very different from Community design and from the UK registered design, it may be present in respect of many designs protected in other ways.

Subsistence

The following key statutory provisions indicate just how different the UK unregistered design right is from other forms of design protection. It should be studied and compared to the basic requirements for subsistence of Community design. It is clear that originality is first considered in a copyright sense before looking at whether the design is **commonplace**.

KEY STATUTE

Section 213(1), (2) and (4) Copyright, Designs and Patents Act 1988

'(1) Design right is a property right which subsists in accordance with this Part in an original design.

(2) In this Part 'design' means the design of any aspect of the shape or configuration (whether internal or external) of the whole or part of an article.

. . .

(4) A design is not 'original' for the purposes of this Part if it is commonplace in the design field in question at the time of its creation.'

KEY DEFINITION: Commonplace

The word 'commonplace' was new to English law when introduced by the Directive protecting semiconductor topographies in 1986. There are a number of judicial statements, none of which are entirely satisfactory. They include:

- '. . . any design which is trite, trivial, common-or-garden, hackneyed or of the type which would excite no peculiar attention in those in the relevant art is likely to be commonplace'
- 'What really matters is what prior designs the experts are able to identify and how much those designs are shown to be current in the thinking of designers in the field at the time of creation of the design in question'.

It is important to note, however, that a design which has become very familiar does not necessarily become 'commonplace'. For example, if a design is applied to an article made by one manufacturer which sells in large numbers, that does not necessarily mean it is commonplace.

Exceptions to subsistence of UK unregistered design right

KEY STATUTE

Section 213(3) Copyright, Designs and Patents Act 1988

'Design right does not subsist in −

(a) a method or principle of construction,

(b) features of shape or configuration of an article which −

   (i) enable the article to be connected to, or placed in, around or against, another article so that either article may perform its function, or

   (ii) are dependent upon the appearance of another article of which the article is intended by the designer to form an integral part, or

(c) surface decoration.'

The first exception, methods or principles of construction, is unlikely to be relevant in the vast majority of cases. The exceptions in section 213(3)(b)(i) and (ii) are often referred to as the 'must-fit' and 'must-match' exceptions. Surface decoration is also excepted, this being the proper subject matter of copyright. An example of surface decoration is a willow pattern applied to a dinner plate.

KEY CASE

Dyson Ltd v *Qualtex (UK) Ltd* **[2006] RPC 31, CA**

Concerning: Various aspects of design right including the scope of the 'must-fit', 'must-match' and surface decoration exclusions

Facts

The defendant supplied duplicate spare parts (pattern parts) for the claimant's vacuum cleaners. The claimant sued on the basis of unregistered design rights subsisting in the design of the parts of its vacuum cleaners.

Legal principle

The 'must-fit' exclusion does not mean that the articles have to physically touch. A clearance between them, if it allows one article to perform its function, may be within the exclusion. The exclusion may apply where the two articles are designed sequentially, one after the other.

For 'must-match' exclusion it is design dependency which is important. The more room there is for design freedom, the less likely the exception will apply.

The reason for the surface decoration exclusion was because it was protected by copyright. Surface decoration could be applied to a two-dimensional article or three-dimensional article or to a flat surface of a three-dimensional article. Surface decoration was not limited to something applied to an existing article and it could come into existence with the surface itself. Surface decoration could itself be three-dimensional, such as beading applied to furniture. However, a feature having a function, such as ribbing on the handle of a vacuum cleaner, was unlikely to be surface decoration. This had a function of helping provide grip.

A design must qualify for protection and may qualify by virtue of the design, the commissioner (if commissioned) or employer (if created by an employee). It may also qualify by virtue of the person who first markets articles to the design in the European Community if it does not otherwise qualify. These provisions are mirrored in those concerning first ownership of the design right.

✓ Make your answer stand out

Demonstrate that you understand the similarities and differences between the four forms of design rights. Even if not specifically asked, where appropriate mention other rights that could subsist in a design. For example, in a question on Community design, mention that either or both forms of UK design rights might subsist and/or artistic copyright (briefly explaining why). Also consider the pros and cons between the various forms of protection (an obvious example being that registration affords monopoly protection).

■ Putting it all together

Answer guidelines

See the essay question at the start of the chapter.

Approaching the question

Consider the nature of the Community design and the reasons for having both an RCD and UCD – then focus on the UCD. Note that the UK unregistered design right is very different and identify the main differences, particularly in relation to subsistence and duration.

Think about the implications, for example, noting that because of the overlap in some cases, that an unregistered UK design may have longer protection than permitted under the Community Design Regulation. Consider whether and how the UK system could be changed, for example, to mirror that under the Community Design Regulation.

Important points to include

■ The question asks for a critical discussion so your answer should go beyond the mere descriptive.

■ It would be useful to first set out the relevant provisions in the Community Design Regulation whilst seeking to reflect on the underlying policy for the scheme under the Regulation.

■ Remembering that the question is concerned with the scheme of protection under the Community Design Regulation, this requires consideration of the rules for registrability (or subsistence in the case of the unregistered Community design), the scope of protection, the rights of the owner and limitation of those rights.

■ Identify and discuss the equivalent aspects of the UK unregistered design right, noting that it is quite different from the Community design, and critically analyse and comment on to what extent and how they conflict with the scheme under the Community Design Regulation.

■ An example of this is that an unregistered design may be protected for only three years under the Community design, yet the same design *may* be protected in the UK by the unregistered design right for up to 15 years (bearing in mind of course that the overlap between the two forms of protection is by no means complete because of the different rules for subsistence and, for the UK unregistered design right, qualification requirements).

■ Other examples include the fact that additional damages may be available for infringement of the UK unregistered design right and there are no limitations to the rights equivalent to those for Community design, for example, teaching, experimentation and repairing ships and aircraft.

✓ **Make your answer stand out**

Having addressed the conflicts between the Community design and the UK unregistered design right, construct and support an argument about whether the UK unregistered design right ought to be repealed, for example, on the basis that it is now unnecessary or confuses the issues of protection of designs.

It might impress an examiner to note that the Community design is not without its problems, for example the protection of graphic symbols and typefaces which may also be protected by copyright law. Unless such designs are registered, giving monopoly protection, there is little point in the Community design for them. Furthermore, as the period of protection for the unregistered Community design commences when first made available to the public, the UK approach of basing duration on the end of the calendar year of creation is arguably more certain.

READ TO IMPRESS

Carboni, A. (2008) 'Design validity and infringement: feel the difference' 30(3) *EIPR*, 111.

Cornwell, J. (2013) 'Dyson and Samsung compared: functionality and aesthetics in the design infringement analysis' 35(5) *EIPR*, 273.

Forsyth, E. (2008) 'Infringement of a registered Community design: a landmark decision by the English Court of Appeal' 22(1) *World Intellectual Property Report*, 33.

Hartwig, H. (2010) '*GrupoPromer* v *OHIM and PepsiCo* (T-9/07): the General Court's first decision on a Community design's validity – all's well that ends well?' 32(9) *EIPR*, 419.

Michaels, A. (2006) 'The end of the road for pattern spare parts? *Dyson Ltd* v *Qualtex (UK) Ltd*' 28(7) *EIPR*, 396.

www.pearsoned.co.uk/lawexpress

Go online to access more revision support including quizzes to test your knowledge, sample questions with answer guidelines, podcasts you can download, and more!

Trade mark registrability

8

Revision checklist

Essential points you should know:

- [ ] The meaning of a sign
- [ ] How a sign can be represented graphically
- [ ] The absolute grounds for refusal of registration
- [ ] The relative grounds for refusal of registration
- [ ] What is an identical or similar mark and what are identical or similar goods or services
- [ ] The definition of consumer
- [ ] How the consumer will perceive the marks and goods
- [ ] How the likelihood of confusion is assessed
- [ ] What will amount to a mark with a reputation
- [ ] What constitutes without due cause, unfair advantage and detriment

■ Topic map

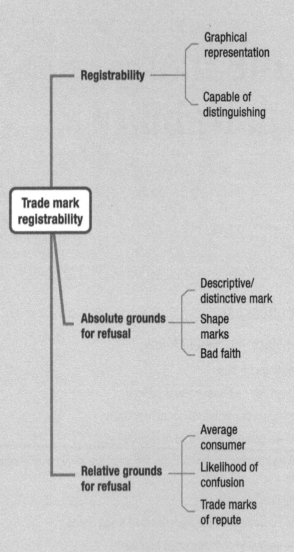

- **Registrability**
  - Graphical representation
  - Capable of distinguishing

- **Trade mark registrability**

- **Absolute grounds for refusal**
  - Descriptive/ distinctive mark
  - Shape marks
  - Bad faith

- **Relative grounds for refusal**
  - Average consumer
  - Likelihood of confusion
  - Trade marks of repute

A printable version of this topic map is available from **www.pearsoned.co.uk/lawexpress**

■ Introduction

The primary purpose of a trade mark is to distinguish the goods or services of one undertaking from those of other undertakings.

Trade marks are a badge of origin and may have great economic value. They are the most harmonised of the intellectual property rights in the European Union. The Trade Marks Act 1994 implemented the First Council Directive to approximate the laws of Member States relating to trade marks (since replaced by Directive 2008/95/EC of the European Parliament and of the Council of 22 October 2008 to approximate the laws of the Member States relating to trade marks: hereinafter, the 'trade marks Directive').

A trade mark is registered under a class of good or services initially for a period of ten years but it can then be renewed every ten years as long as it is being used in the appropriate class. You must use it or lose it. It is a property right which arises on registration and can be licensed or sold. It is enforceable by the owner or licensee of the right. However, not only can a trade mark be used to help a business in furtherance of its trade but it can also protect consumers from being deceived into buying the wrong or even counterfeit goods or services.

ASSESSMENT ADVICE

Essay questions

You may be asked to discuss the policy reasons for refusing the registration of a trade mark. This will entail dealing with the absolute grounds of refusal with discussion on the distinctive rather than descriptive nature of a trade mark. This ground prevents proprietors from monopolising marks that should be free for all to use. You will also have to examine the relative grounds where registered marks are protected against the use by rival traders dealing in the same or similar goods or services, leading to confusion in the mind of the consumer. There is no confusion needed where extra protection is given to an existing sign which has a reputation. Such signs are vulnerable to free riding, and detriment may occur if a subsequent similar mark is registered even for dissimilar goods. This gives extremely strong protection to the proprietor of the right. The reasons for this additional protection may need to be analysed.

Problem questions

Whether a mark can be represented graphically sounds like a simple question but difficulties can arise when you are attempting to register colour, shape, smell and ▶

sound marks. Although there may not always be a full problem question on this area, it may well come into the discussion of any issues surrounding registrability and there may be an essay question on the problems associated with registering such marks.

Sample question

Could you answer this question? Below is a typical problem question that could arise on this topic. Guidelines on answering the question are included at the end of this chapter, whilst a sample essay question and guidance on tackling it can be found on the companion website.

PROBLEM QUESTION

Toys Ltd has created a new night-time toy of unusual shape which could only be described as an alien hedgehog. The toy when warmed by the heat of a child's body gives off a chocolate smelling sleeping gas which causes the child to fall into an uninterrupted night's slumber. The hedgehog shape provides a considerable surface area so that a sufficiently large dose of the gas can escape even if the toy is being tightly cuddled. The toy is a luminous puce colour.

Advise Toys Ltd as to the likelihood of success in registering the colour, smell and shape of their toy.

Registrability of trade marks

KEY DEFINITION: Trade marks – basic requirements for registration

A mark will only be registered as a trade mark if it is a sign, if it can be represented graphically and if it is capable of distinguishing one trader's goods or services from those of another.

KEY STATUTE

Article 2 of the trade marks Directive (see also s. 1 of the Trade Marks Act 1994)

'A trade mark may consist of any sign capable of being represented graphically, particularly words, including personal names, designs, letters, numerals, the shape of goods or of their packaging, provided that such signs are capable of distinguishing the goods or services of one undertaking from those of other undertakings.'

Thus the shape of a bottle or a person's name can all be regarded as signs and on the face of it are registrable as **trade marks**. However, even though they qualify as a sign, they will only be registrable if they are capable of graphical representation and *also* capable of distinguishing the goods or services of one undertaking from those of other undertakings. An obstacle in the registration of shapes, sounds and other unusual types of signs is that the public has not tended to perceive such signs as trade marks. Note that the Directive uses the term 'undertaking' rather than the now rather old-fashioned English word 'trader'. The Trade Marks Act 1994 also uses the term 'undertaking'.

Graphical representation

! Don't be tempted to . . .

Don't forget that there are serious problems with the graphical representation of colour, sound, taste and smell marks. A mark must be advertised in the *Trade Marks Journal* so that other traders know what marks are registered and they can avoid infringing them. If the representation of the marks is not certain, clear, precise and durable, traders cannot know if they are infringing another's mark. With regard to smell marks in particular it may be impossible to even ascertain what the trade mark is despite detailed descriptions and chemical formulae being provided. Such marks are unlikely to be accepted.

KEY CASE

Case C-283/01 *Shield Mark BV* v *Joost Kist* [2003] ECR I-14313, ECJ
Concerning: whether a sound mark can be represented graphically

Facts

This was a failed application 'to register the first 9 notes of Beethoven's "Für Elise"' along with the musical stave depicting the notes plus the designation 'the crowing of a cock', also described using the Dutch word *Kukelekuuuuuu.*

Legal principle

Representation will only be accepted if clear, precise, self-contained, easily accessible, intelligible, durable and objective.

In *Shield Mark* the musical notes and stave were found to be insufficiently precise. If there had been more detail provided so that in addition to the notes the stave was divided into measures with a clef, rests and accidentals, this would have been sufficiently precise to be registered. The legal principle that the graphical representation of a mark must be clear, precise, etc. is also applicable to determining whether colour, smell, taste and shape marks are adequately graphically represented. See *Société des Produits Nestlé SA* v *Cadbury UK Ltd* [2013] EWCA Civ 1174 for an example of a colour mark that failed the clarity and precision test.

Capable of distinguishing

Once you have established that a mark is capable of graphical representation the next requirement that must be met is that it must be capable of distinguishing the goods or services of one undertaking from those of other undertakings. More explanation of this is found under Article 3 of the trade marks Directive (section 3 of the Trade Marks Act 1994).

■ Absolute grounds for refusal

KEY STATUTE

Article 3(1)(a) to (d) of the trade marks Directive (see s. 3(1)(a) to (d) Trade Marks Act 1994)

'(1) The following shall not be registered . . .

(a) signs which cannot constitute a trade mark [i.e. they do not satisfy the requirements of Article 2];

(b) trade marks which are devoid of any distinctive character;

(c) trade marks which consist exclusively of signs or indications which may serve, in trade, to designate the kind, quality, quantity, intended purpose, value, geographical origin, or the time of production of goods or of rendering of the service, or other characteristics of goods or services;

(d) trade marks which consist exclusively of signs or indications which have become customary in the current language or in the bona fide and established practices of the trade; . . .'

Article 3(3) of the trade marks Directive (see the proviso to s. 3(1) Trade Marks Act 1994)

'A trade mark shall not be refused registration or be declared invalid in accordance with paragraph 1(b), (c) or (d) if, before the date of application for registration and following the use which has been made of it, it has acquired a distinctive character . . .'

Article 3(3) thus provides for the registration of signs as trade marks which, although within the exceptions to registration under Article 3(1)(a) to (d), have in fact acquired a distinctive character through use.

Descriptive/distinctive mark

KEY DEFINITION: Descriptive mark

A descriptive mark describes the goods or services in question and so cannot distinguish the goods or services of one undertaking from those of other undertakings, for it is applicable to all such goods.

The mark must not be *devoid* of **distinctive** character, meaning it must not be *wholly* **descriptive** such as 'Eurolamb' for lamb coming from Europe. It must have some aspect that will make it distinctive. In addition, the mark must not be used to describe the quality or characteristics of the goods, for example 'best', 'woolly', 'Cotswold Stone', 'vintage' or 'smokeless' or which have become common in the relevant trade to describe the goods or services for which registration is sought. This is intended to protect others who may honestly wish to use such marks in their own trade.

KEY DEFINITION: Distinctive mark

A mark that is distinctive is capable of distinguishing the goods or services of one undertaking from those of other undertakings.

You must note the caveat that if, although apparently lacking in distinctive character, the mark has acquired distinction through use, it may be registered. It must still satisfy the requirement of Article 2 of being capable of distinguishing. If it were a very common word, such as 'treat', it would be unlikely to succeed but if the public has been educated by prolonged advertising, as in 'Have a break' used in relation to the chocolate bar KitKat, there may be a finding of distinctiveness through use.

✎ EXAM TIP

For the best marks in an essay you must demonstrate not just legal knowledge but an awareness of the reasons behind the legislation. Keep in mind that purely descriptive signs should not be monopolised by one undertaking but should be kept available for all traders to use. Descriptive marks will not be registered, despite the fact that defences may be available to honest traders who use such marks. Also remember that a sign may be made up of more than one aspect. As long as the descriptive part of the mark is not the most dominant part, the additions may help it to acquire a distinctive character.

We are still left with the problem of whether a mark which primarily has a descriptive character, such as being a geographical name, can become distinctive through use.

KEY CASE

Joined Cases C-108/97 and C-109/97 *Windsurfing Chiemsee Productions* v *Huber and Attenberger* [1999] ECR I-2779, ECJ

Concerning: whether a geographical name can become distinctive through use

Facts

This was an application by a sportswear company situated near Lake Chiemsee to register the name 'Chiemsee' which it had used for some time for its sportswear.

Legal principle

Geographical names are on the face of it unregistrable. They are descriptive and for public policy reasons they need to be kept available for all to use. However, if the name has acquired distinction as a mark through use, it is acceptable to register it as long as it is not being or is unlikely to be used in the future by other traders for that type of good or service.

✓ **Make your answer stand out**

There is tension between the decisions in *Windsurfing* and *Baby Dry* when using descriptive or laudatory terms. Ilanah Simon (2003) explores this area. Make your answer stand out by explaining that these cases conclude either that marks should not be registered if not viewed as a badge of origin or, alternatively, that there is a need to keep some trade marks available for the use of other traders.

Shape marks

A shape mark must be quite unusual to be regarded as distinctive. Neither the Lindt Bunny nor the KitKat shape is regarded as distinctive despite long use.

KEY STATUTE

Article 3(1)(e) of the trade marks Directive (see s. 3(2) Trade Marks Act 1994)

'3(1) The following shall not be registered . . .

    (e) signs which consist exclusively of –

        (i) the shape which results from the nature of the goods themselves,

        (ii) the shape of goods which is necessary to obtain a technical result, or

        (iii) the shape which gives substantial value to the goods.'

Unlike the other exceptions above, signs caught by Article 3(1)(e) cannot be registered even if they have achieved distinctiveness through use.

A shape mark must not result *exclusively* from the nature of the goods. Consequently one may not register the basic shape of a tyre or a simple shape of a rugby ball (a particularly distinctive tread pattern for a tyre or stitching pattern for a ball may be registrable). As far as the technical result exclusion, it may apply even if there are other ways of obtaining that result, as in *Philips* v *Remington* (below).

The shape must not give *substantial value* to the goods. So if you buy a particular good for its shape rather than to acquire that type of good itself, this will be excluded. Does the shape have an intrinsic value that attracts buyers who purchase the product to which it is applied because of that shape? An example might be a sculpture hewn out of stone. It is felt that if registration of such shapes were granted it would create a monopoly in those shapes and as a result a monopoly in the goods themselves. Compare with copyright which does not prevent the independent creation of another shape which turns out to be very similar by coincidence.

KEY CASE

Case C-299/99 *Koninklijke Philips Electronics* v *Remington Consumer Products Ltd* [2002] ECR I-5475, ECJ

Concerning: the registrability of a functional shape mark

Facts

Philips sued for infringement of its pictorial trade mark which showed the shape of a three-headed rotary shaver. In response, the validity of the mark was called into question as being a shape necessary to obtain a technical result.

Legal principle

The purpose of the provision is to prevent people obtaining exclusive rights over technical developments. Consequently, the mark will not be registered even if there is another way of obtaining the same end result. The test is – was it that shape due to its function?

✎ EXAM TIP

To get a good mark you should show that you understand the consequence of a different decision. If the court had accepted that registration would be allowed for a shape mark with a technical function as long as there was another way of obtaining the same result, the provision would in effect have been made pointless. An unlimited monopoly would have been created over that way of doing something.

Bad faith

KEY STATUTE

Article 3(1)(f) and (g) of the trade marks Directive (see s. 3(3) Trade Marks Act 1994)

'3(1) The following shall not be registered . . .

(f) trade marks which are contrary to public policy or to accepted principles of morality;

(g) trade marks which are of such a nature as to deceive the public, for instance as to the nature, quality or geographical origin of the goods or service; . . .'

Article 3(2)(d) of the trade marks Directive (see s. 3(6) Trade Marks Act 1994)

'3(2) Any Member State may provide that a trade mark shall not be registered . . . where and to the extent that: . . .

(d) the application for registration of the trade mark was made in bad faith by the applicant.'

Note: This provision was optional. It was implemented in the UK.

A mark will not be registered if it is contrary to public policy or to accepted principles of morality. However, keep in mind that public policy and the moral principles of right-thinking members of the public may change with time. Cases on this topic must be read in light of the morals of society at the time the case was heard.

A mark will not be registered if it is deceptive: for example, indicating an item is made of wool when it is in fact made of polyester, that it had been made in a particular location when it had not or it is of a protected emblem. An application to register a UK trade mark (and in other Member States under their harmonised national trade mark systems) will be denied if made in **bad faith**. This does not apply to a Community trade mark but bad faith is a ground for invalidity of a Community trade mark.

Bad faith can have various meanings. Lack of intention to use the mark will show bad faith, and attempting to register a mark to which it is known another is entitled is a relevant but not sufficient factor (see the *Yakult* case (Case C-320/12) [2013] ETMR 36). Such attempt could be to cash in on another's reputation or to prevent another trader from registering it. Although intention is important, the applicant does not have to believe that what they were doing was wrong.

KEY DEFINITION: Bad faith

Bad faith is behaviour falling short of acceptable standards of commercial behaviour. It must be assessed objectively and case by case.

Once the hurdles of the absolute grounds for refusal have been overcome, it is then time to consider other undertakings that may have marks which could be affected by the granting of a new trade mark.

Relative grounds for refusal

KEY STATUTE

Article 4(1)(a) of the trade marks Directive (see s. 5(1) Trade Marks Act 1994)

'(1) A trade mark shall not be registered . . .

(a) if it is identical with an earlier trade mark, and the goods or services for which the trade mark is applied for . . . are identical with the goods or services for which the earlier trade mark is protected.'

Identical signs may not be registered for identical goods. No confusion is required by the consumer for refusal of registration on these grounds (it can be taken to be presumed as a matter of law). A sign will be held to be identical to a trade mark where it reproduces, without any modification or addition, all the elements constituting the trade mark or where, if viewed as a whole, it contains differences so insignificant that they may go unnoticed by an **average consumer**.

Average consumer

KEY DEFINITION: Average consumer

The average consumer is taken to be a consumer of the goods concerned who is reasonably well informed, reasonably observant and circumspect (careful).

KEY STATUTE

Article 4(1)(b) of the trade marks Directive (see s. 5(2) Trade Marks Act 1994)

'(1) A trade mark shall not be registered . . .

(b) if because of its identity with, or similarity to, the earlier trade mark and the identity or similarity of the goods or services covered by the trade marks, there exists a likelihood of confusion on the part of the public; the likelihood of confusion includes the likelihood of association with the earlier trade mark.'

A trade mark will not be registered if:

- the mark is either identical or similar to an earlier mark;
- it is registered in relation to goods or services which are either similar or identical to the earlier mark;
- and there is a likelihood of confusion on the part of the consumer.

□ REVISION NOTE

Go to Chapter 9 and make sure that you understand the connection between registrability and infringement.

How the likelihood of confusion is assessed

The likelihood of confusion must be appreciated globally. You must take into account the visual, aural and conceptual similarities of the marks. You must bear in mind their distinctive and dominant components. A lesser degree of similarity between the marks may be offset by a greater similarity between the goods (or services), and vice versa. There is a greater likelihood of confusion where the earlier trade mark has a highly distinctive character, either because it is a very unusual mark, or because it has become highly distinctive through use.

The average consumer normally perceives a mark as a whole and does not analyse its various details. It is the initial impact that counts. If the earlier mark is very distinctive either because it is very unusual or it has become very well known, consumers are likely to think of it on seeing a similar mark and become confused. However, you must also keep in mind the way the consumer perceives a mark. Are they likely to see it or hear it? Two marks when spoken may sound similar, but, if the consumer will only see the mark and not hear it spoken, it is the visual aspect you must consider and which must lead to confusion.

KEY CASE

Case C-342/97 *Lloyd Schuhfabrik Meyer & Co. GmbH* v *Klijsen Handel BV* [1999] ECR I-3819, ECJ

Concerning: confusion in relation to a trade mark

Facts

Lloyds was the claimant's mark for shoes. The mark was distinctive through use. The defendant, Klijsen, manufactured similar goods under the Loint's brand.

Legal principle

The more similar the goods and the more distinctive the earlier mark, the more likely there is to be confusion on the part of the consumer.

> **❗ Don't be tempted to . . .**
>
> Don't mix up who must be confused and what they must be confused about. Applying the tests of similarity, confusion, etc. to a given fact situation can be a challenge but it is wise to remain heedful that it is the consumer whose likely confusion must be established. Mere association is not sufficient unless this association leads to confusion as to origin. The consumer must believe that the goods came from the same undertaking or economically linked undertakings. It will help if you keep in mind that although communication, investment and advertising are secondary functions of a trade mark the basic and primary function of a trade mark is an indicator of origin.

Trade marks of repute

KEY STATUTE

Article 4(3) of the trade marks Directive

'4(3) A trade mark shall . . . not be registered . . . if it is identical with, or similar to, an earlier Community trade mark . . . and is to be . . . registered for goods or services which are not similar to those for which the earlier Community trade mark is registered, where the earlier Community trade mark has a reputation in the Community and where the use of the later trade mark without due cause would take unfair advantage of, or be detrimental to, the distinctive character or the repute of the earlier Community trade mark.'

Note: Article 4(4)(a) of the trade marks Directive permitted Member States to apply this ground for refusal of registration also in respect of earlier national trade marks. The UK chose to implement this option. For the UK provisions, see section 5(3) of the Trade Marks Act 1994 which applies to earlier Community and national trade marks.

Originally, this provision related only to identical or similar marks and non-similar goods or services. The latest codified version of the trade marks Directive retains this provision as originally expressed. However, in Case C-292/00 *Davidoff & Cie SA* v *Gofkid Ltd* [2003], the Court of Justice ruled that the provision also applied to identical or **similar goods or services**. The UK Trade Mark (Proof of Use, etc.) Regulations 2004/946 changed the UK Act accordingly. There is no requirement for confusion in this provision but there must be some link made by the consumer between the two marks. The first thing that must be established in order to take advantage of this provision is that the earlier trade mark has a reputation among a substantial part of the public in a significant part of the territory at issue.

KEY DEFINITION: Similar goods or services

Goods or services are similar if they are in competition; if the consumer would buy one instead of the other.

KEY CASE

Case C-375/97 *General Motors* v *Yplon* [1999] ECR I-5421, ECJ

Concerning: who must know of and how aware must they be of a trade mark for it to be a mark with a reputation

Facts

General Motors was the proprietor of the mark 'Chevy' for motor vehicles which objected to Yplon registering the mark 'Chevy' for detergents and cleaning materials.

Legal principle

The mark must have acquired a reputation with a substantial part of the relevant public in a significant part of the territory, but who the public are depends on the product. The market share, intensity of sale, geographical location and duration of use and the advertising of the mark must all be considered.

Once you have established that the mark has a reputation you must then prove that the mark is being used without due cause. There should be no overriding reason why the new mark must be used. It may also take unfair advantage of the mark with a reputation: that is, use showing a disregard for the standards of acceptable commercial behaviour leading to increased sales of the new mark. Alternatively, use of the new mark may cause blurring, the lessening of the capacity of the famous mark to identify and distinguish goods, dilution which is the gradual whittling away of the identity of the mark in the mind of the public by its use on other goods, or tarnishment, detracting from the appeal of the existing mark, probably by some unsavoury connotation.

■ Putting it all together

Answer guidelines

See the problem question at the start of the chapter.

Approaching the question

Make sure you state the issues and identify the rules, cases and statutes. You then apply the relevant law to the facts using arguments on both sides and then finally advise.

Important points to include

- Explain that in order to register a trade mark it must comply with the requirements of Article 2 of the Directive (s. 1 of the Act) and Article 3 (s. 3) and the sign must be capable of graphic representation and of distinguishing the goods of one undertaking from those of another undertaking.

- Advise as to whether the colour puce, applied to the type of good for which the mark is to be used, would be regarded as a badge of origin having acquired distinction through use.

- The registration of smell and colour marks must be discussed with reference to the requirements laid out in *Shield Mark*. The mark must be clear, precise, self-contained, easily accessible, intelligible, durable and objective. Here reference to an internationally recognised colour code such as Pantone would be expected. Ask, would a third party, when seeing the descriptions used, understand precisely what the mark was?

- Assess how likely it is that consumers will see the hedgehog shape as a badge of origin, the fundamental purpose of a trade mark, or whether they will merely regard it as the good itself.

- Shape marks which result from the nature of the goods and are necessary to obtain a technical result or give substantial value to the goods themselves are excluded from registration. These must be discussed with reference to *Philips* v *Remington* and the functional aspect of the shape of the toy.

> ✓ **Make your answer stand out**
>
> Make your point that you are not tempted to fall into a trap. Show that you recognise that, although a mark will not be registered if it is contrary to public policy, it must be the mark that causes the outrage, not the product. Here the purpose of the toy, anaesthetising children to sleep, may be distasteful but the effect of the gas is not the subject of registration.

READ TO IMPRESS

Bainbridge, D.I. (2004) 'Smell, sound, colour and shape trade marks: an unhappy flirtation?', March, *JBL*, 219.

Howell, C. (2007) 'Intel: a mark of distinction', 29(11) *EIPR*, 441.

Simon, I. (2003) 'What's cooking at the CFI? More guidance on descriptive and non-descriptive trademarks', 25(7) *EIPR*, 322.

Trimmer, B. (2009) 'The power of attraction: do trade marks have an "image" problem in the English courts?', 31(4) *EIPR*, 195.

Walmsley, M. (2007) 'Too transparent? ECJ rules Dyson cannot register transparent collection chamber as a trade mark', 29(7) *EIPR*, 298.

Wood, I. and Bagnall, M. (2013) 'Colour marks: a purple decision clears the way forward' 35(5) *EIPR*, 300

www.pearsoned.co.uk/lawexpress

Go online to access more revision support including quizzes to test your knowledge, sample questions with answer guidelines, podcasts you can download, and more!

Trade mark infringement

9

Revision checklist

Essential points you should know:

- [ ] The meaning of an identical sign
- [ ] Whether use of a trade mark must be in the course of trade
- [ ] In what circumstances a trade mark can be used to compare one trader's goods or services with those of another
- [ ] The limits of the own name defence
- [ ] What will amount to descriptive use
- [ ] When a registered trade mark may be used to indicate the intended purpose of another's goods or services
- [ ] What constitutes a groundless threat of infringement proceedings

■ Topic map

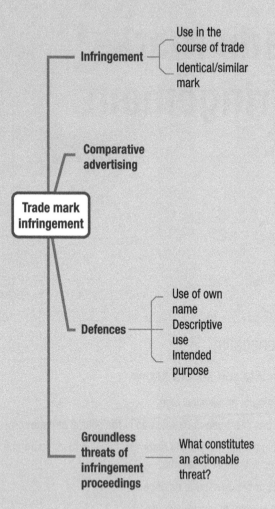

A printable version of this topic map is available from **www.pearsoned.co.uk/lawexpress**

■ Introduction

A trade mark gives the proprietor the exclusive right to use that mark in respect to the goods or services for which it has been registered.

Infringement can extend to the spoken use of words as well as to graphic representation. The relative grounds of refusal of registration and the acts that amount to infringement are very similar but infringement is concerned with the use of a sign, whereas the relative grounds for refusal are concerned with conflict with an earlier trade mark. Apart from case law on use of a sign in the course of trade or use of a sign in a trade mark sense, case law on the relative grounds for refusal is exchangeable and applicable to actions on infringement. An application to register a trade mark can be opposed on the basis of earlier trade marks, including UK or **Community trade mark** and earlier well-known trade marks entitled to protection under the Paris Convention for the Protection of Industrial Property 1883 or the Agreement establishing the World Trade Organization 1994. However, infringement under the Trade Marks Act 1994 can only apply to use of signs within the UK which conflict with trade marks having effect in the UK: that is, the UK registered trade mark and the Community trade mark.

ASSESSMENT ADVICE

Essay questions

An essay question may well ask about the issues of use and the difference between use of a trade mark to describe a good or service and use in the trade mark sense.

Problem questions

Remember that a problem question on this topic could include problems of jurisdiction as well as infringement itself. You must also be careful to consider whether any defences might affect your answer.

■ Sample question

Could you answer this question? Below is a typical essay question that could arise on this topic. Guidelines on answering the question are included at the end of this chapter, whilst a sample problem question and guidance on tackling it can be found on the companion website.

The 11th recital of the preamble to the trade marks Directive (2008/95/EC, codified version) states that the function of a trade mark is in particular to guarantee the trade mark as an indication of origin, and that protection is absolute in the case of identity between the mark and the sign and between the goods or services concerned and those for which the mark is registered.

Critically discuss this statement in the light of the Court of Justice ruling in Case C-206/01 *Arsenal Football Club plc* v *Reed* [2002] ECR I-10273.

■ Infringement

Use in the course of the trade

Article 5(1)(a) of the trade marks Directive (s. 10(1) Trade Marks Act 1994)

'(1) ... the proprietor shall be entitled to prevent all third parties not having his consent from using in the course of trade:

    (a) any sign which is identical with the trade mark in relation to goods or services which are identical with those for which the trade mark is registered.'

When talking about infringement under the Trade Marks Act 1994, remember that there must be genuine use of the sign as registered. Using a registered figurative mark in combination with a registered word mark can amount to genuine use (see *Specsavers* case C-252/12 CJEU). Use must be use within the UK (or on a website directed at trade in the UK) and, furthermore, that use must be in the course of trade. Although not flagged up in either the Act or the Directive, there is an issue as to whether the use in question has to be 'trade mark use'. Does trade mark use mean any use in commerce, such as a photograph of a footballer in his football shirt with his team logo or the use of AdWords in a search engine provider such as Google? (AdWords are advertising keywords used to secure an entry in a sponsored list of hits following the entry of a trade mark in a search engine.)

Case C-206/01 *Arsenal Football Club plc* v *Matthew Reed* [2002] ECR I-10273, ECJ

Concerning: whether the use of a sign as a badge of support or loyalty created a sufficient impression of a connection as to amount to infringement of a trade mark as 'trade mark use' indicating origin

Facts

Arsenal Football Club had registered the names 'Arsenal' and 'Gunners' along with the club emblems for goods such as scarves and sports clothing. Mr Reed, under a disclaimer pointing out that they were unlicensed, sold similar goods with the club's names and emblems attached. The club claimed trade mark infringement but Mr Reed retorted that he was not using the club's mark in a 'trade mark sense'.

Legal principle

The issue is not whether there has been trade mark use. What is at issue is whether the use of the mark created the impression to the consumer, not necessarily the purchaser, that there was a material link with the proprietor (any disclaimer may not have been seen post sale). Unchecked use of the mark by a third party which is not descriptive use is likely to damage the main function of the mark because it could no longer guarantee origin. The fact here that the mark was a badge of allegiance was irrelevant.

Use needs to be in a form that indicates the origin of the goods or services or use which affects the interests of the proprietor of the mark in some other form such as the investment or advertising function of the trade mark.

You should deal with any question involving this issue by asking whether there is commercial use which undermines the proprietor's interest. To show that you have a good understanding of the whole topic you should point out that, even if regarded as initially infringing, if the facts allow there may be a defence if the mark is being used descriptively: Article 6(1) of the trade marks Directive (s. 11(2)(b) of the Act) or the hosting defence may apply to internet service providers under Article 14(1) of the Directive on electronic commerce (2000/31/EC): see Schrijvers (2011).

Although used commercially by search engine providers, the use of trade marks as keywords (such as Google AdWords) are not necessarily regarded as use by them indicating origin. The advertiser on the site will be regarded as using the AdWords in a way that has an adverse effect on the origin function of the trade mark unless they make it clear to a significant proportion of reasonably well-informed consumers before they click on the site that the goods or services supplied on their website do not come from the trade mark proprietor but that they are supplying alternative goods.

✓ **Make your answer stand out**

Nigel Parker (2006) considers the cases of *Arsenal* v *Reed*, where the ECJ decided that 'trade mark use' was not an essential requirement for infringement to be found, and *R* v *Johnstone* where 'trade mark use' was held to be essential to a finding of infringement. Parker explains that Lord Nicholls in *Johnstone* concluded that the retailer of bootleg recordings of the Bon Jovi pop group ('Bon Jovi' being a registered trade mark) had not intended to use the name as a trade mark but only as a description of the goods. Consequently the bootleg recordings did not infringe. Make your answer stand out by explaining that Nigel Parker argues that this conclusion 'flatly contradicts the decision in *Arsenal* v *Reed*' where it was held that neither confusion nor 'trade mark use' are required in a case where a third party's use threatens a trade mark's essential distinctive functions, and that such diametrically opposed interpretations by the House of Lords are highly undesirable.

Identical/similar mark

In order to infringe another's mark under Article 5(1)(a) of the Directive (s. 10(1) of the Act), the defendant must be using an **identical mark**. Does this mean the mark must be exactly the same?

❗ **Don't be tempted to . . .**

Don't forget that the difference between what is an identical mark and what is a similar mark can be tricky. Although similar marks are not identical marks, the Court of Justice of the European Union (formerly ECJ) has used the concept of imperfect recollection in determining whether an almost identical sign is identical to the registered trade mark. This creates a blurring between what is an identical sign, where no confusion need be proved, and what amounts to a similar sign where confusion must be established. Keep this distinction in mind.

If a sign is identical to a registered mark and the goods or services for which it is being used are identical, no confusion on the part of the consumer need be proved. Infringement will have occurred. If there is mere similarity in the marks and in the goods or services, evidence of likely confusion on the part of the consumer is needed in order to prove infringement. It is therefore important to know whether marks are identical or similar so that you know whether or not you need to prove that confusion has occurred.

KEY DEFINITION: Identical marks

The average, reasonably well-informed, observant and circumspect customer assessing the mark globally may not notice the addition of a hyphen or an apostrophe, especially when they are apart, but would notice the inclusion of an extra word, if the word would not go unnoticed by the average consumer.

KEY CASE

Case C-291/00 *LTJ Diffusion SA* v *Sadas Vertbaudet SA* [2003] ECR I-2799, ECJ
Concerning: meaning of identical mark

Facts

The claimant was a clothing company with the trade mark 'Arthur' in a distinctive handwritten form. The defendant sold children's clothing by mail order and applied for a Community Trade Mark 'Arthur et Félicie'. The claimant objected to the defendant's use of the mark and had opposed the CTM application.

Legal principle

'. . . a sign is identical to a trade mark where it reproduces, without any modification or addition, all the elements constituting the trade mark or where, viewed as a whole, it contains differences so insignificant that they may go unnoticed by an average consumer'.

There may be a successful infringement action where there is incomplete identity of the mark and the goods or services but where there is a likelihood of confusion on the part of the consumer as to source. If a mark has a reputation and there is an identical or similar sign and goods or services which are either similar or dissimilar, there may be a finding of infringement without any confusion. There must, however, be some link made in the mind of the consumer and there must also be a finding of unfair advantage or damage to the repute of the mark. In addition, the defendant must have no justification of due cause for use of the mark with a reputation.

📖 REVISION NOTE

Apart from the fact that the mark must be used in the UK, the requirements of Article 5 of the Directive (s. 10 of the Act) and Article 4 of the Directive (s. 5 of the Act) are almost identical. These provisions should therefore be read in conjunction with the discussion on the provisions on the relative grounds for refusal in Chapter 8.

▊ Comparative advertising

Although not found in some other states of the European Union, honest and fair **comparative advertising** is permitted in the UK both under the Trade Marks Act 1994 and in the light of the Directives relating to misleading advertising (Directive 97/55/EC amending Directive 84/450/EEC).

KEY DEFINITION: Comparative advertising

Comparative advertising is the use of a competitor's trade mark to highlight the comparative advantage of one's own rival goods or services.

KEY STATUTE

Directive 84/450 concerning misleading advertising as amended by Directive 97/55

Comparative advertising shall be permitted when it does not create confusion between the advertiser and a competitor, discredit or denigrate the trade mark/names, take unfair advantage of the reputation of a trade mark or present goods or services as imitations or replicas of those bearing a protected mark.

From this we can see that a trader may use what is undisputedly the trade mark of a rival on identical goods or services. This use of a rival's mark is only allowed as long as the use made of the mark does not fall within the misleading advertising Directive.

❗ Don't be tempted to . . .

Don't overlook the non-essential functions of a trade mark. Even where the use made of the mark does not jeopardise the essential function of a trade mark, to guarantee the origins of the goods or services, comparative advertising may still be prohibited if other functions of the trade mark such as communication, investment and advertising are affected.

Case C-87/07 *L'Oréal SA* v *Bellure NV* [2009] ECR I-5185, ECJ

Concerning: whether a competitor's use of a proprietor's trade mark when comparing goods constituted infringement

Facts

Bellure sold cheap imitations of L'Oréal's luxury perfumes and published lists comparing them. The bottles and packaging were similar but there was no likelihood of confusion as the Bellure perfumes were sold under different names.

Legal principle

Article 5(1)(a) of the trade mark Directive entitles a trade mark proprietor to prevent the use of their trade mark by a third party where the comparative advertisement does not satisfy the requirements of Article 3a(1) of Directive 84/450/EEC.

There is an assumption that comparative advertising should be allowed. However, by imitating the perfumes of L'Oréal, even though they were telling the truth, Bellure was held to be riding on the coat-tails of the famous mark. It was taking unfair advantage of the reputation of the well-known mark by presenting its goods as imitations or replicas contrary to Article 3a of the misleading advertising Directive (as amended): see Horton (2011).

Defences

Practical considerations are important when considering defending any alleged trade mark infringement. A defendant must make sure that it is worth defending their actions. Establishing a defence could cost a great deal of money and may be unsuccessful. It may be more sensible to give an undertaking not to continue to use the sign.

Article 6(1) of the trade marks Directive

'A registered trade mark is not infringed by –

(a) the use by a person of his own name and address,

(b) the use of indications concerning the kind, quality, intended purpose, value, geographical origin, the time of production of goods or rendering of services, or other characteristics of goods or services, or

(c) the use of the trade mark where it is necessary to indicate the intended purpose of a product or service (in particular, as accessories or spare parts) provided the use is in accordance with honest practices in industrial or commercial matters.'

Use of own name

The provision states that as long as the use does not amount to passing off (see Chapter 10), the defence will apply to the use of a natural person's own name. It has also been accepted for full company names but not the name of one of the company's directors. It would seem, therefore, that there would be nothing to stop a person changing their name to that of a successful competitor and then pleading this defence. You must, however, ask yourself, would this be regarded as an honest practice?

KEY CASE

***Asprey and Garrard Ltd v WRA (Guns) Ltd* [2002] FSR 31, CA**

Concerning: the use of a newly adopted company or trading name

Facts

A family business was sold along with the trade mark Aspreys, but a member of the Asprey family and ex-employee of the company then began to use his name as a trade name for similar luxury goods.

Legal principle

The 'own name' defence does not apply to the names of new companies or new trade names, as otherwise the route to piracy would be obvious.

Descriptive use

Some parts of this defence may on the face of it seem irrelevant. Article 3 of the Directive (s. 3 of the Act) should have prevented marks such as those which indicate the kind or quality of goods from being registered. If the mark, however, was not exclusively descriptive or it had acquired distinction through use, registration might have been allowed. This defence may then be needed to protect an honest trader who wishes to use such a word in their own business. There is a debate about whether some types of use are descriptive use, needed in order to let the consumer know the various characteristics of the goods, or infringing use.

☐ REVISION NOTE

Please refer back to Chapter 8 for further discussion of the descriptive and distinctive issue.

KEY CASE

Bravado Merchandising Services Ltd v Mainstream Publishing (Edinburgh) Ltd
[1996] FSR 205, CSOH
Concerning: the use of a trade mark as a description of the goods

Facts

The name of the pop group Wet Wet Wet had been registered as a trade mark. A book was written about the group and the name of the group was used in the title.

Legal principle

The defence is available when all the characterisations of infringement are present, not so that a mark can be used in a trade mark sense but for pure descriptive use which conveys features or characteristics of the product concerned.

✎ EXAM TIP

Please note that the question whether the use is descriptive or as a trade mark will only need to be addressed if infringement has first been established. If you are dealing with a problem question and you have found infringement, it is worth looking to see whether there is anything in the facts you have been given to raise such a defence. The problem of whether the use is descriptive or as a trade mark may then need to be discussed. Remember that although detriment does not have to be proved, use must be in accordance with honest practices in industrial or commercial matters. Keep in mind that what is regarded as honest commercial practice may change over time.

Intended purpose

This defence to an infringement action facilitates free competition. A garage which repairs BMW cars needs to use the BMW logo to advertise the fact that it offers that service. This defence allows such necessary and honest use of the trade mark.

KEY CASE

Case C-228/03 *Gillette Company v LA-Laboratories Ltd Oy* **[2005] ECR I-2337, ECJ**
Concerning: whether the use of the trade mark to indicate the intended purpose was 'necessary' and honest

Facts

Gillette Company had a registration for the trade marks 'Gillette' and 'Sensor' for razors. LA-Laboratories made razors and blades sold under the trade mark Parason Flexor, and sold blades with a sticker applied to their packaging which stated, 'All Parason, Flexor and Gillette Sensor handles are compatible with this blade'. ▶

> **Legal principle**
>
> Use of the trade mark was *necessary* if it was the only way in practice to allow the public to understand the intended purpose for that product. However, the use must not give the impression that there is a commercial connection or reduce the trade mark's value by affecting its distinctive character or by denigrating the mark. Nor must the use indicate that it is a replica of the product bearing the trade mark.

■ Groundless threats of infringement proceedings

Having infringement proceedings brought against a business can be very disruptive. It can involve an injunction, search and seizure orders and other such remedies. This gives a great deal of power to the claimant which can be abused. To prevent this happening the **groundless threats** procedure was incorporated into the Trade Marks Act 1994 (see Chapter 6 for groundless threats in relation to patents). There is no EU equivalent, although groundless threats actions are possible in the UK in relation to Community trade marks.

> **KEY DEFINITION: Groundless threat**
>
> No matter how ambiguous or indecisive, a communication will be regarded as a threat if understood by the ordinary recipient of the communication to be a threat to bring infringement proceedings.

Any person affected by a threat made without due cause can apply to the court and seek a declaration that the threat is unjustified, and an injunction to prevent further threats and damages. This is particularly useful to small retailers.

> **KEY STATUTE**
>
> **Section 21 Trade Marks Act 1994**
>
> Any person aggrieved may bring proceedings for relief where there has been an unjustified threat to bring proceedings for infringement of a registered trade mark. The relief sought can be an injunction, damages or a declaration that the threats are unjustifiable. The mere notification that a trade mark is registered does not constitute a threat of proceedings. This section does not, however, apply to the importation of goods, where the mark has been applied to goods or their packaging, or to the supply of services under the mark.

What constitutes an actionable threat?

❗ Don't be tempted to . . .

Don't forget about unjustified threats. It may be tempting to advise a proprietor whose mark has been infringed to start proceedings immediately against the infringer. This may not, however, always be the best advice. Keep in mind that if unjustified threats of legal proceedings are made this can lead to unpleasant consequences. A threat can be in a letter or it can be spoken. It may be express or implicit. Such threats are usually but not necessarily made by letter. Mere notification of the existence of the trade mark will not constitute a threat. If, however, a communication in whatever form is meant to unnerve the recipient or make them seriously think that what they are doing, if continued, may result in proceedings being brought, that will constitute a threat (see Silver and Smith 2011).

KEY CASE

L'Oréal (UK) Ltd v *Johnson & Johnson* [2000] FSR 686, ChD
Concerning: what amounts to a threat to bring proceedings

Facts

The claimants' solicitors wrote to the defendant asking whether infringement proceedings of the defendant's marks 'would be brought by reason of their use of similar words for similar products'. The letter in reply contained an enigmatic message but mentioned the possibility in the future of proceedings for infringement.

Legal principle

The test as to whether a communication amounted to a threat was whether it would be understood by the ordinary recipient in the position of the claimant as constituting a threat of proceedings for infringement.

■ Putting it all together

Answer guidelines

See the essay question at the start of the chapter.   ▶

Approaching the question

You have been asked to critically discuss this statement. You must explain the relevant ideas and examine both sides of the argument. Come to a judgement about their strengths and weaknesses through reasoned argument supported by authority.

Important points to include

- You have been asked to address a particular aspect of infringement so do not construct your answer in a way that is a summary of the whole topic.

- This question is concerned with Article 5(1)(a) (s. 10(1) of the Act) and the use of an identical sign in relation to identical goods. There is no requirement of confusion so this does not need to be discussed. The focus should be upon the mark being used in the course of trade.

- There has been much debate about whether use in the course of trade must be use as a 'trade mark'. Briefly outline the issues.

- A comparison of the approaches taken by Laddie J and the ECJ in *Arsenal* would be wise. Laddie J concentrated upon the perception of the consumer as to 'trade mark use' while the ECJ stated that whether there had been 'trade mark use' was not the appropriate question. The essential issue was whether the use made of the mark had affected the proprietor's interests, having regard to the trade mark's functions.

- The ECJ did not consider either the opinions of the consumer or the infringer when deciding whether the proprietor's interests had been affected.

- Most descriptive use would not affect the proprietor's interest (*Bravado Merchandising*) but it would of course depend on the facts of each case.

✓ Make your answer stand out

This issue raises wider policy considerations such as a fear that intellectual property can create an unfair monopoly. Demonstrating an awareness of this will gain you a better mark, as will referring to the consequences of the different approaches to 'trade mark use' (see Parker 2006) alluding to the uncertainty in this area created by the House of Lords in *Johnstone*.

READ TO IMPRESS

Blythe, A. (2013) 'Searching questions: issues surrounding trade mark use on the internet' [2013] 9 *EIPR*, 507.

Horton A. 'The implications of *L'Oreal* v *Bellure* – a retrospective and a looking forward: the essential functions of a trade mark and when is an advantage unfair?' [2011] 9 *EIPR*, 550.

Isaac, B. and Joshi, R. (2005) 'What does identical mean?', 5 *EIPR*, 184.

Parker, N. (2006) 'A raw deal for performers: Part 2 – Anti-piracy', 7 *Entertainment Law Review*, 204.

Schrijvers, M. (2011) 'European Court rules on the position of eBay regarding sale of infringing products: *L'Oréal* v *eBay*', 11 *EIPR*, 723.

Silver, J. and Smith, J. (2011) 'Court of Appeal allows appeal in threats case – trap for the unwary: *Best Buy Inc.* v *Worldwide Sales Corp. Espana SL*', 10 *EIPR*, 662.

www.pearsoned.co.uk/lawexpress

Go online to access more revision support including quizzes to test your knowledge, sample questions with answer guidelines, podcasts you can download, and more!

10

Passing off

■ Topic map

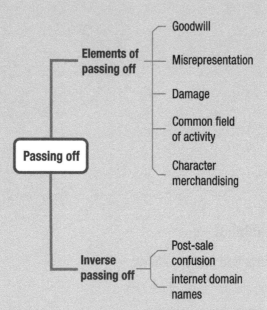

■ Introduction

Nobody has any right to present their goods as the goods of somebody else.

Passing off is a tort developed out of deceit. It can be described as the common law form of trade mark law but it is wider than trade mark law. Passing off can be used to prevent damage not only to distinctive names, numbers and devices but also to colours, the style of advertising campaigns, shapes and packaging. Passing off protects the property right in the goodwill of a business, not a mark itself. The goodwill is usually in the UK. Actual or likely damage, such as the diversion of business or damage to reputation, exposure to litigation or erosion of the mark, is a requirement for the commission of the tort. There must have been a false representation, intentional or unintentional, coming from the defendant, either verbally or by use of a name, get-up or logo which causes confusion in the mind of the customer or potential customer. The claimant's actual identity does not need to be known to consumers. It is generally accepted that regardless of the fact that customers may be misled, honest use of one's own name is permitted, but such use must not be made in a way that would exaggerate the connection.

ASSESSMENT ADVICE

Essay questions

Passing off lends itself to essay questions. It is a tort that was created to encourage fairness and honesty among traders and it requires that the public be deceived (confused). However, as the attributes of the public have changed over time, so too might the outcome of particular cases and this change can be analysed with reference to any policy issues or development in other areas of law such as trade marks.

Problem questions

It is important to identify all the issues raised in a problem question. But keep in mind that the basic requirements needed for a passing-off action to succeed must all be present. Once you have identified the issues, then apply the relevant authority to them and decide whether you have indeed got what amounts to the tort of passing off or, if not, why not.

■ Sample question

Could you answer this question? Below is a typical problem question that could arise on this topic. Guidelines on answering the question are included at the end of this chapter, whilst a sample essay question and guidance on tackling it can be found on the companion website.

PROBLEM QUESTION

Two months ago Mr Raz took part in a popular television programme where entrepreneurs attempt to gain investment from rich businessmen. Mr Raz won a substantial investment for his 'Koconut Sauce', a high-quality tangy sauce to be used with savoury dishes marketed in a coconut-shaped plastic bottle. Mr Raz had created a song called 'I am a Koca-koca Nut' which he sang on the television programme and which has since been used in an extensive advertising campaign to promote the sauce. An extended version of the advertisement has been released as a music video and has been a great success. The video features Mr Raz playing his guitar sitting under a coconut tree while surrounded by bottles of the sauce. The sauce is marketed in most supermarket chains.

Betty runs an organic burger bar called Betty's Burgers. The bar has a reputation for home-made produce. Betty has put up a large sign in her shop saying 'Put coconut sauce on your Betty Burger'. Betty has the video of Mr Raz as background music playing almost non-stop in her burger bar. She has registered the domain name coconutsauce.co.uk and has started taking orders online to supply organic food shops with her coconut sauce.

Advise Mr Raz as to whether he could bring a successful passing-off action against Betty.

■ The elements of passing off

The 'classic trinity' requirements for a finding of **passing off** are:

- the existence of the claimant's **goodwill**;
- a misrepresentation as to the goods or services offered by the defendant; and
- damage (or likely damage) to the claimant's goodwill as a result of the defendant's misrepresentation.

KEY DEFINITION: Passing off

Passing off is an attempt by trader B to take advantage of the goodwill established by trader A, to the detriment of trader A.

Goodwill

KEY DEFINITION: Goodwill

Goodwill is the attractive force attached to the name, get-up or logo which brings in custom.

Passing off does not protect the mark itself but the goodwill associated with the mark. In order to attract goodwill the mark, get-up or logo must be distinctive of the claimant's goods or services. Otherwise it would be impossible to show that goodwill was associated specifically with the claimant's mark rather than that of any other trader. On the face of it a descriptive word, get-up or logo is not distinctive and therefore is incapable of attracting goodwill. It may, however, become distinctive if used in an unusual or unexpected context or if it has become distinctive through exclusive use by the claimant.

KEY CASE

Reckitt & Colman Products Ltd v *Borden Inc.* [1990] 1 All ER 873 (*Jif Lemon* case) HL

Concerning: use of a deceptively similar but descriptive 'get-up'

Facts

The claimant sold Jif lemon juice in a plastic lemon-coloured and lemon-shaped receptacle. The defendant sold lemon juice in a similar but not identical container.

Legal principle

Although each case in passing off depends on its own particular facts, the existence of the claimant's extensive and exclusive goodwill built up over many years, a misrepresentation as to the goods or services offered by the defendant, and damage (or likely damage) to the claimant's goodwill as a result of the defendant's misrepresentation, amounted to passing off.

Although the *Jif Lemon* case is authority for the 'classic trinity' of goodwill, misrepresentation and damage, the *Advocaat* case is the first major case setting out the basic requirements for success in a passing-off action. This case demands a misrepresentation made by a trader in the course of trade to prospective or ultimate customers of goods or services supplied by them which is calculated to injure the business or goodwill of another trader and which causes actual damage. This case also raised an issue as to whether consumers had to be deceived into buying the wrong goods or services or whether dilution or erosion amounted to passing off.

KEY CASE

Erven Warnink Besloten Vennootschap v *J Townend & Sons Ltd* [1979] AC 731 (*Advocaat* case) HL

Concerning: whether passing off could result even if consumers did not mistakenly buy the wrong goods

Facts

Substantial loss of sales was suffered by a well-known and popular liqueur called Advocaat due to a similar but cheaper and inferior-quality drink called 'Keeling's Old English Advocaat' being placed on the market. The case was unusual in that a number of Dutch traders collectively had goodwill in the name 'Advocaat'.

Legal principle

Not only damage due to lost sales but damage to reputation by being associated with an inferior product amounted to passing off and traders either individually or as a class could be protected from deceptive use of their name by competitors.

Reputation is not the same as goodwill. A trader can have a reputation but carry out no business in this country. Traditionally there must be some business or market in the UK for goodwill to exist. The time taken to develop goodwill and the extent of the area affected are fact dependent, as is the ownership of the goodwill itself. Goodwill, the ability to pull in customers, is of value because of its power to promote future businesses which can include the ability to attract licence fees. The acquisition and durability of goodwill is an area of law that develops as business practices change. With greater use of the internet, advertising and globalisation, goodwill can spread faster and wider in the future, but for passing off there must still be goodwill in the UK rather than a mere reputation (see Wadlow 2011).

KEY CASE

Scandecor Development AB v *Scandecor Marketing AB* [1999] FSR 26, CA

Concerning: whether a parent or subsidiary company owns the goodwill in a name

Facts

A Swedish poster-producing company was split and set up a UK subsidiary trading under the name Scandecor which was the sole retailer in the UK. The UK company continued to obtain its posters from the Swedish company.

Legal principle

The goodwill belongs to the company that either traded or exercised business control over activities in the UK.

Misrepresentation

KEY DEFINITION: Misrepresentation

A misrepresentation is a false description made consciously or unconsciously by the defendant. Such representation can be implied by the use of a mark, trade name or get-up with which the goods of the claimant are associated in the minds of a substantial number of ordinary, sensible members of the public who have been or are likely to be misled due to the representation.

Deception due to **misrepresentation** is an essential element for a finding of passing off. Merely demonstrating that as a result of the similarities between two marks people may be confused does not mean there is passing off, while adding a disclaimer will not necessarily prevent a finding of passing off.

KEY CASE

Arsenal Football Club plc v Reed [2001] RPC 46, ChD

Concerning: use of identical marks on identical goods

Facts

The defendant had, for over 30 years, sold memorabilia bearing the football club's name and logo. However, due to a disclaimer the defendant's customers realised that the goods neither came from nor were sanctioned by the club. They bought his products as badges of allegiance to the football club.

The disclaimer Mr Reed displayed on these facts was sufficient to prevent the misrepresentation necessary for passing off; it was, however, insufficient to prevent consumers making a material link when the case was referred to the ECJ on the trade mark infringement issue.

Legal principle

For passing off to have occurred customers or ultimate consumers must have been deceived such that there exists a real likelihood of confusion.

✎ EXAM TIP

Although many of the concepts used in the trade marks statutes are similar to those found in passing off, the two are distinct. You must make sure that you do not combine them in your discussions. You may find that an examination question contains issues that relate to both passing off and trade marks, but you must keep these issues separate and deal with them independently.

Damage

Being unable to register your name as a company or domain name, diversion of business, damage to reputation, exposure to litigation or erosion of the mark can all amount to damage.

KEY CASE

Taittinger SA v Allbev Ltd [1993] FSR 641, CA

Concerning: whether 'extended' passing off can be found due to erosion of goodwill even when there is no confusion in the mind of the consumer

Facts

The defendant, an English company, made a cheap non-alcoholic drink called Elderflower Champagne and although no confusion was alleged the growers of the sparkling wine objected to the use of the word Champagne.

Legal principle

Erosion of the distinctiveness of the name with a reputation is an actionable form of damage to the goodwill of the business of the claimant.

Common field of activity

A common field of activity is no longer an essential requirement of passing off. However, lack of some similarity in the field creates a presumption that confusion and therefore passing off has not occurred. The public are unlikely to make a connection and be misled in the absence of a common field of activity unless the goods or services are in effect household names.

Character merchandising

! Don't be tempted to . . .

Don't be quick to assume that passing off has occurred in character merchandising situations. Character merchandising is the licensing of mainly fictional characters. If goodwill has been established in the character and the name is used by another trader, passing off could arise. However, a lack of a common field of activity can present a problem with such character merchandising. Use of the name Wombles for rubbish skips was held not to be passing off because it did not compete with the owner of the name who traded in licensing children's television characters.

There have been developments in this area. They are, however, confined to circumstances where the public can be shown to be conscious of merchandising in the particular field. This awareness will make them more likely to assume mistakenly that there has been a licence or sponsoring agreement entered into for the use of a personality's name or image. For other character merchandising, where no such assumption is likely to be made, it is still unlikely that a passing-off action will succeed.

KEY CASE

Irvine v *Talksport Ltd* [2003] FSR 35, ChD

Concerning: whether falsely implying that a celebrity has endorsed a product is actionable under passing off

Facts

The defendant ran the radio station 'Talk Radio'. They used a doctored photograph of Eddie Irvine, the Formula One Grand Prix racing driver, in a promotional campaign, having substituted a portable radio clearly displaying the words 'Talk Radio' for a mobile phone.

Legal principle

Celebrities may have a proprietary right in the goodwill of their name or image and that right can be protected by bringing an action in passing off. Despite there being no common field of activity the public may nevertheless assume falsely that the product had been endorsed by the claimant.

 Make your answer stand out

Make your answer stand out by explaining that until *Irvine* v *Talksport* the requirement of a common field of activity had traditionally been a barrier to celebrities using passing off to prevent their name or image being used by others. Gary Scanlan (2003) criticises the extension of passing off as in effect having no authority, claiming that what the courts appear to be doing is creating a 'personality right' and that monopolies of this type should not be created for policy reasons. You could comment on what appears to be the extension of a UK image right in light of the successful claim in passing off by Rihanna the pop star against the sale of t-shirts depicting her image by Topshop (*Fenty* v *Arcadia Group* [2013] EWHC 2310 (Ch)).

■ Inverse passing off

Inverse passing off occurs where the defendant falsely claims that the claimant's goods or services are actually made or provided by the defendant.

Inverse passing off is the opposite of traditional passing off where trader B tries to take the customers of trader A by pretending that their goods are the goods of trader A. With inverse passing off trader B pretends that trader A's goods are in fact trader B's. There can be no lost sales due to buyers confusing the defendant's products (or services) with those of the claimant, but there can be damage to trader A if the defendant's product is inferior to the claimant's product and buyers mistakenly think that the defendant's product is that of the claimant.

KEY CASE

Bristol Conservatories Ltd v *Conservatories Custom Built Ltd* **[1989] RPC 455, CA**
Concerning: inverse passing off

Facts

The defendant's sales representatives showed potential customers photographs of conservatories as a sample of the defendant's workmanship. The photographs were, in fact, of the claimant's conservatories.

Legal principle

This misdescription harmed the claimant's goodwill and constituted passing off.

Post-sale confusion

Post-sale confusion is where the misrepresentation comes after the goods have been purchased.

Even if there is no deception at the time of sale, later confusion as to the origin of the name, mark or device can still damage the goodwill by a process of dilution or erosion. Although UK cases have not regarded **post-sale confusion** as amounting to passing off, there has been an extension of passing off in other jurisdictions (see *Levi Strauss & Co.* v *Kimbyr Investments Ltd*).

Bostick Ltd v *Sellotape GB Ltd* **[1994] RPC 556, ChD**

Concerning: whether a get-up which could only be seen post sale could lead to passing off due to erosion of goodwill

Facts

The claimant sold blue adhesive putty called 'Blu-tack' and the defendant sold a similar blue product called 'Sellotak', but the blue could only be seen after purchase and removal from its packaging.

Legal principle

As the defendant's product could not be seen at the point of sale, there was no danger of confusion.

Passing off and internet domain names

Although not the typical application of passing off, it has been successfully pleaded concerning the wrongful use of domain names. If a third party without due cause registers company A's trading name as a domain name, this will prevent company A from registering the name itself and will constitute damage to company A. Such 'cybersquatting' cases have usually included an offer to sell the domain name to company A for an inflated price.

Marks & Spencer plc v *One in a Million Ltd* **[1998] FSR 265, CA**

Concerning: whether registering as a domain name the name of another's company with associated goodwill constituted passing off

Facts

The defendants had registered a number of names including 'bt.org' but had not made any use of the domain names in the course of trade.

Legal principle

It was sufficient for passing off for a person to put an 'instrument of deception' into the hands of another or to authorise another to do so.

For such an action to succeed there must still be proof of damage or a likelihood of damage and this will be difficult to show if the claimant has chosen a descriptive or generic name for their business, such as Radio Taxis for a taxi cab business.

📖 REVISION NOTE

It is important to remember that passing off can be used in conjunction with trade mark infringement or where for some reason a trade mark application has not been made or a trade mark has been lost. (Please refer to Chapters 8 and 9 on these aspects of trade marks.)

■ Putting it all together

Answer guidelines

See the problem question at the start of the chapter.

Approaching the question

To begin with you must:

- identify the relevant issues to establish whether Mr Raz has goodwill in his name, mark or get-up;
- then determine whether there has been a misrepresentation and what damage may have ensued.

Important points to include

- Two months is a relatively short time to establish goodwill, but the publicity surrounding his television appearance would help to establish it.
- His goodwill would be attached to the name, get-up and the song but are they distinctive enough to be protected?
- The name of the sauce: Koconut spelt with a K is not totally descriptive but would this K be obvious to the average consumer?
- The shape of the bottle is part of the get-up but is it too descriptive?
- Would the distinctive spelling of the sauce be recognised in the song, which would be heard rather than seen?
- Will the customers have been deceived (confused) by any misrepresentation?
- Look at the use made of the sauce, on all savoury dishes in comparison to burgers only. Is there a common field of activity?
- The Koconut sauce is sold in supermarkets but not Betty's Bar so would there be confusion at point of sale?

- Betty's Burger Bar has a reputation for home-made produce.
- The spelling of her sauce is purely descriptive.
- Customers will see the spelling in a written form rather than hear it sung.
- Betty is serving the sauce in her bar and selling via the internet rather than in a supermarket.
- She has registered the domain name but is using it in the furtherance of her own business rather than as an instrument of deception.
- What damage do you think Mr Raz has suffered or could suffer? Damage does not have to be lost sales but could be damage to reputation or even exposure to litigation. (Health and safety is important with food.)

✓ **Make your answer stand out**

Make your reader aware that passing off cannot be used to prevent competition. It can be used only to prevent the use of another's goodwill to their detriment.

READ TO IMPRESS

Carty, H. (2012) 'Passing off: frameworks of liability debated' 2 *IPQ*, 106

Harrold, L. (2006) 'Beyond the well-trodden paths of passing off: the High Court decision in *L'Oréal* v *Bellure*', 5 *EIPR*, 304.

Moscona, R. (2006) 'The sale of business goodwill and the seller's right to use his own name', 2 *EIPR*, 106.

Scanlan, G. (2003) 'Personality, endorsement and everything – the modern law of passing off', 12 *EIPR*, 563.

Sims, A. (2004) 'Rethinking one in a million', 10 *EIPR*, 442.

Wadlow, C. (2011) '*Hotel Cipriani Srl* v *Cipriani (Grosvenor Street) Ltd* [2010] EWCA Civ 110; [2010] RPC 16', 1 *EIPR*, 54.

www.pearsoned.co.uk/lawexpress

Go online to access more revision support including quizzes to test your knowledge, sample questions with answer guidelines, podcasts you can download, and more!

161

11

Intellectual property, computer software and the internet

Revision checklist

Essential points you should know:

☐ The provisions in the Directive on the legal protection of computer programs concerning subsistence, rights and exceptions.

☐ Ownership issues in relation to computer programs and other works created by consultants and other 'non-employees'.

☐ The two forms of protection afforded to databases by the Directive on the legal protection of databases (copyright and the *sui generis* database right) and Court of Justice cases on the scope of the database right.

☐ Case law on non-textual copying of computer programs and the exceptions to the permitted acts under the Directive on the legal protection of computer programs.

☐ The exceptions to the meaning of 'invention' relevant to computer-implemented inventions.

☐ Approaches to these exceptions by the UK courts and the Boards of Appeal of the European Patent Office.

☐ The impact of trade marks in relation to the internet and online sales and implication of the use of trade mark words by others such as competitors, for example, as AdWord keywords.

■ Topic map

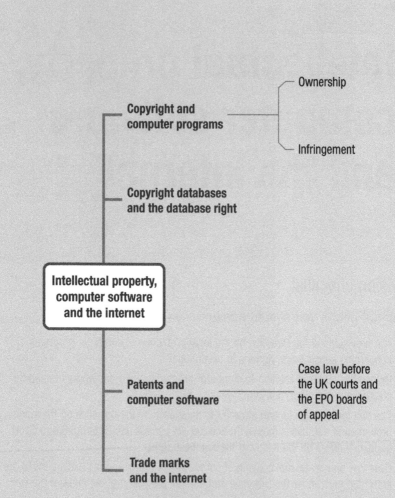

Copyright and computer programs
- Ownership
- Infringement

Copyright databases and the database right

Intellectual property, computer software and the internet

Patents and computer software
- Case law before the UK courts and the EPO boards of appeal

Trade marks and the internet

A printable version of this topic map is available from **www.pearsoned.co.uk/lawexpress**

■ Introduction

Computer software and, in particular, computer programs have pushed the boundaries of intellectual property law and resulted in numerous legal initiatives.

You should be aware of how copyright and patent law apply to computer programs, databases and other works in digital form. Another issue is the use of another's trade marks in advertising on the internet. Many lecturers like to test these areas which can, at first sight, seem daunting to students. Don't forget that computer programs and databases have immense commercial value. You should not let the technology put you off – it's just that when it comes to computer software, different rules apply. You should bear in mind that copyright has specific provision for protecting computer programs and databases and also protects copy-protection systems in respect of all forms of digital works including film and music. There is also a form of protection for 'right-management information' applied to digital works, such as copyright notices and terms and conditions under which the work can be accessed, downloaded or copied. Whilst copyright embraces computer software under its protection regime, you should contrast this to patent law which seems to exclude computer programs and business methods, etc. executed digitally. However, these things may be protected if there is some 'technical effect'. You should note that the case law on this is unsatisfactory and still in a state of flux. As with intellectual property generally, you should always watch for and keep abreast with new developments.

ASSESSMENT ADVICE

Essay questions

Essay questions often ask students to consider the relative merits of the copyright and patent system as a means of protecting computer programs. You should consider the strengths and weaknesses of both systems of protection in the context of computer programs. For example, the fact that copyright does not provide monopoly protection whereas determining the state of the art for computer-implemented inventions is difficult and unpredictable.

Problem questions

You may be asked to advise on the non-textual copying of computer programs or the scope of protection of databases by the database right in a particular scenario. In the case of the former, you should notice that there are no specific legislative provisions ▶

but important case law, especially *SAS Institute* v *World Programming Ltd.* In the case of the database right, you should apply the provisions of the Database Directive (or the UK Regulation, although the Directive is best) and important case law before the Court of Justice such the *British Horseracing Board* v *William Hill*.

■ Sample question

Could you answer this question? Below is a typical essay question that could arise on this topic. Guidelines on answering the question are included at the end of this chapter, whilst a sample problem question and guidance on tackling it can be found on the companion website.

ESSAY QUESTION

Small and medium sized enterprises (SMEs) have made outstanding contributions to the development of computer technology in the past but they are ill-served by a patent system which gives disproportionate benefits to large corporations with the financial resources to enable them to obtain and aggressively use their software patent portfolios. Discuss.

■ Copyright and computer programs

Computer programs, including their preparatory design material, are a form of literary work.

📖 REVISION NOTE

Refer to the basic rules on the subsistence of copyright in relation to literary works, set out in Chapter 1. Don't forget that a computer program, including its preparatory design material, is a literary work.

> **KEY STATUTE**
>
> **Article 1, Directive 2009/24/EC on the legal protection of computer programs (codified version)**
>
> '(1) . . . the term "computer programs" shall include their preparatory design material.
>
> (2) Protection . . . shall apply to the expression in any form of a computer program. Ideas and principles which underlie any element of a computer program, including those which underlie its interfaces, are not protected by copyright . . .
>
> (3) A computer program shall be protected if it is original in the sense that it is the author's own intellectual creation. No other criteria shall be applied to determine its eligibility for protection.'

The provisions of the Copyright, Designs and Patents Act 1988 use different language compared with the Directive (for example, the Act simply states that a computer program must be original but there is no reference to the author's own intellectual creation, unlike the case with copyright databases). Students should note these differences but be aware that, unless optional or a derogation, the provisions in the Directive take precedence and will usually be referred to by judges.

The scope of the restricted acts and the exceptions to infringement for computer programs are set out in the Directive (again, subject in some case to a rewrite in the Copyright, Designs and Patents Act 1988). The restricted acts are:

- the temporary or permanent reproduction by any means and in any form, in part or in whole;

- the translation, adaptation, arrangement and any other alteration of a computer program and the reproduction of the results thereof;

- any form of distribution to the public including rental of the original or copies.

The doctrine of exhaustion of rights applies so that the copyright owner cannot object to the further distribution of a copy of the computer program he has sold. However, he retains the right to object to further rental of that copy.

There are specific exceptions to the restricted acts that apply to computer programs.

> **KEY STATUTE**
>
> **Article 5, Directive 2009/24/EC on the legal protection of computer programs (codified version)**
>
> '(1) [reproduction, translation, adaptation etc. if necessary for the purpose of error correction providing this is not prohibited by express contractual provision.]
>
> (2) The making of a back-up copy by a person having a right to use the computer program may not be prevented by contract in so far as it is necessary for that use. ▶

> (3) The person having a right to use a copy of a computer program shall be entitled . . . to observe, study or test the functioning of the program in order to determine the ideas and principles which underlie any element of the program if he does so while performing any of the acts of loading, displaying, running, transmitting or storing the program which he is entitled to do.'

A licensee or other person having the right to use a computer program also has the 'right' to decompile that computer program if indispensable to obtain the information necessary to achieve the interoperability of an independently created computer program with that program or another program, provided such information has not previously been readily available to such persons (Article 6 of the Directive on the legal protection of computer programs).

KEY CASE

Case C-406/10 *SAS Institute Inc.* v *World Programming Ltd*, 2 May 2012, CJEU

Concerning: writing new computer programs to emulate the operation and functions of existing computer programs

Facts

The defendant acquired the claimant's computer programs under a 'Learning Edition' licence.

By closely observing, studying and testing the claimant's programs, the defendant was able to write new computer programs to carry out the same functions and to use the same language so that users could write their own programs to carry out their own statistical analysis applications. The learning edition licence prohibited the use of the claimant's software to write competing software.

Legal principle

The observing, studying and testing permitted act applied to the defendant's work in writing new programs as it had not copied the code of the claimant's computer programs but carried out those acts to access the underlying ideas and principles which are not protected by copyright. Furthermore, the terms in the licence agreement which attempted to prevent or restrict this were null and void under Article 9 of the Directive on the legal protection of computer programs.

Ownership

Rules as to the first ownership of copyright in a computer program are the same as other original works, but the nature of the software industry means that many computer programs and other items of software are created by consultants and self-employed persons.

Infringement

There are no significant issues with respect to duplicate copying of computer programs but non-textual copying can cause difficulties, such as where an alleged infringer has written a new computer program to emulate the operational and functional aspects of an existing program without copying the code of the existing program.

✓ Make your answer stand out

In a case on non-textual copying of computer programs, after applying the case law, your answer would attract higher marks if you noted that the denial of protection to general ideas and vague business methods accords with the Directive on the legal protection of computer programs which states that ideas and principles which underlie any element of a computer program are not protected by copyright under the Directive. Also note that terms prohibiting or restricting observing, studying and testing the functioning of a computer program to determine underlying ideas and principles or the decompilation of a computer program for the purposes of interoperability are null and void.

■ Copyright databases and the database right

A definition of '**database**' applies equally to copyright databases and databases protected by the database right even though the two rights are quite different.

KEY DEFINITION: Database

A database is a collection of independent works, data or other materials which are arranged in a systematic or methodical way and are individually accessible by electronic or other means.

Note that databases may be electronic or otherwise. A card index arranged alphabetically would fall within the definition. Also note that the contents need not themselves be works of copyright (data or other materials) but, if the contents are protected by copyright or other rights, such rights are not prejudiced by the protection of a database as a database.

KEY STATUTE

Article 3(1), Directive 96/9/EC on the legal protection of databases

'. . . databases which, by reason of the selection or arrangement of their contents, constitute the author's own intellectual creation shall be protected as such by copyright. No other criteria shall be applied to determine their eligibility for that protection.'

Article 7(1), Directive 96/9/EC on the legal protection of databases (the *sui generis* database right)

'Member States shall provide for a right for the maker of a database which shows that there has been qualitatively and/or quantitatively a substantial investment in either the obtaining, verification or presentation of the contents to prevent extraction and/or re-utilization of the whole or of a substantial part, evaluated qualitatively and/or quantitatively, of the contents of that database.'

The recitals to the Directive make it clear that the investment referred to for the *sui generis* right is in relation to human, technical and financial resources. For copyright databases, there seems some doubt as to the meaning and scope of the term 'author's own intellectual creation', for example, whether it applies to the intellectual effort and skill in the creation of new data.

KEY CASE

Football Dataco Ltd v *Stan James (Abingdon) Ltd* [2011] RPC 9, ChD
Concerning: Whether annual football fixture lists were intellectual creations

Facts

The claimant created the annual fixture lists for the English and Scottish Premier and football leagues on behalf of the relevant football bodies.

Legal principle

The lists were copyright databases because of the 'very significant labour and skill' used to create the lists. The judge also considered that the work involved was not mere 'sweat of the brow'. However, on appeal, the Court of Appeal referred questions relating to 'author's intellectual creation' to the Court of Justice for a preliminary ruling under Article 267 of the Treaty on the Functioning of the European Union (Case C-173/11).

! Don't be tempted to . . .

Don't think that, in terms of databases, copyright and database right are similar. The database right is quite different and is referred to as a *sui generis* right in the Directive on the legal protection of databases. Even so, both rights may subsist in the same database. However, copyright protection is based on 'intellectual creation' whereas the database right is based on 'substantial investment'. Furthermore, the rules for the scope, entitlement and infringement of the two rights are quite distinct. There are further differences – make sure you know them.

KEY CASE

British Horseracing Board Ltd v William Hill Organisation Ltd [2004] ECR I-10415, Court of Justice

Concerning: Whether the creation of data for inclusion in a database fall within the meaning of 'obtaining' for the purposes of the sui generis *database right*

Facts

The British Horseracing Board maintained a database of racehorses from which lists of runners and riders at horse races were compiled.

Legal principle

The purpose of the Directive was to protect that investment in seeking out and collecting together existing data and not to the act of creating those data.

Note the meaning of 'extraction' (permanent or temporary transfer of all or a substantial part of the contents of a database to another medium by any means or in any form) and 'reutilisation' (any form of making available to the public all or a substantial part of the contents of a database by the distribution of copies, by renting, by online or other forms of transmission, subject to exhaustion of rights). The repeated and systematic extraction and reutilisation of insubstantial parts of the contents of a database may infringe the database right where, cumulatively, these acts amount to the extraction and/or reutilisation of a substantial part of the contents of a database measured qualitatively and/or quantitatively. Displaying some or all of the contents of a database on computer screen is an act of extraction. A transfer of data following an on-screen consultation can be an act of extraction which is not limited to a 'cut and paste' operation.

✓ **Make your answer stand out**

Your understanding of the database right will be enhanced significantly by reading articles on the right, in particular, those addressing the Court of Justice rulings on the interpretation of the database rights. A good example is Kemp, R and Gibbons, C, 'Database right after *BHB* v *William Hill*: enact and repent at leisure' [2006] 22 *CLSR* 493. Before reading such articles, make sure you are familiar with the provisions of the Directive on the legal protection of databases. You will then be equipped to give an impressive answer to essay and problem questions on this important form of intellectual property right.

■ Patents and computer software

Certain things are excluded from the meaning of 'invention' for the purposes of patent law. The list of things is not exhaustive nor is there any deducible common logic between the things excluded. Computer programs, as such, are excluded as are business methods and mental acts. Where there is a 'technical effect', this may overcome the exception but where a computer program only performs other excluded matter, that will not count as a valid technical effect, for example, in the case of a business method implemented by a computer program.

📖 **REVISION NOTE**

Refer to the basic rules on patentability in Chapter 5, in particular the exclusions from the meaning of 'invention' under section 1(2) of the Patents Act 1977 and compare with the equivalent provision under Article 52 of the EPC, below.

KEY STATUTE

Article 52 European Patent Convention

'(1) European patents shall be granted for any inventions, in all fields of technology, provided that they are new, involve an inventive step and are susceptible of industrial application.

(2) The following in particular shall not be regarded as inventions within the meaning of paragraph 1:

(a) discoveries, scientific theories and mathematical methods;

(b) aesthetic creations;

(c) schemes, rules and methods for performing mental acts, playing games or doing business, and programs for computers;

(d) presentations of information.

(3) Paragraph 2 shall exclude the patentability of the subject-matter or activities referred to therein only to the extent to which a European patent application or European patent relates to such subject-matter or activities as such.'

Make sure you know which provisions of the European Patent Convention should be equivalent to those in the Patents Act 1977. For example, Article 52(2) and (3) is intended to be equivalent to section 1(2) of the Act. Where you are dealing with such provisions (as is the case with Directives) it is often preferable to go straight to the text of the Convention (or Directive), as senior judges do. Also note that the exceptions in Article 52(2) only apply in as much as the application relates to the excepted matter 'as such'.

Case law before the UK courts and the EPO Boards of Appeal

The single major difficulty is how to interpret the proviso 'as such' in Article 52(3) of the EPC (s. 1(2) of the Patents Act 1977). On this issue, there is some divergence between the Court of Appeal and the EPO Boards of Appeal which have modified their approach to the exclusions since the landmark case of *Vicom*, which itself was followed by the Court of Appeal soon after in cases such as *Fujitsu*.

KEY CASE

Aerotel/Macrossan Patent Application [2007] RPC 7, CA

Concerning: The exclusion from patentability of business methods and computer programs

Facts

This involved two joined cases. Aerotel succeeded in their application regarding a new telephone system where a pre-payment code could be used to make a call from any telephone to the company's exchange, while Macrossan's application failed having been held to be a method of doing business. It merely programmed a machine to ask appropriate questions in order to decide which documents should be used to incorporate a company.

Legal principle

To decide whether this was excluded subject matter, being a computer program or business method 'as such', one must: (1) properly construe the claim; (2) identify the actual contribution (what has the inventor really added to human knowledge?); (3) ask whether it falls solely within the excluded subject matter; (4) check whether the actual or alleged contribution is actually technical in nature. The presence of a technical effect is only to be considered if the invention has passed the first three steps.

The Court of Appeal noted that it was bound by previous Court of Appeal decisions which appear to be narrower than the approach now taken by the EPO Boards of Appeal. However, subsequently in *Symbian Ltd* v *Comptroller-General of Patents* [2009] RPC 1, Lord Neuberger in the Court of Appeal said that a further exception to *stare decisis* could apply where there is a clear decision of the EPO which conflicts with prior UK case law. However, because the law on computer programs at the Boards of Appeal at the EPO was far from settled, Lord Neuberger followed *Aerotel*.

KEY CASE

Hitachi/Auction method [2004] EPOR 548, EPO

Concerning: Whether a computer-implemented method of auctioning was patentable

Facts

The problem solved by the alleged invention concerned delays in submitting bids due to the vagaries and nature of electronic transmission. The solution was to use a Dutch auction method where bidders submitted two bids: their desired bid and maximum bid. After bidding is finished, the result was calculated by setting a price and successively lowering it until the highest desired bid was reached. If there was more than one at the same highest desired bid, the price was automatically increased until the highest maximum price was left from those tying with the same highest desired bids.

Legal principle

A 'non-invention' as such under Article 52(2) would be something which was a purely abstract concept devoid of any technical implications. Consequently, anything performed by a programmed computer (whether claimed in that way, as an entity, or the activity performed by it, has a technical character and is an invention not excluded by Article 52(2). The Board of Appeal said at para 4.6: '. . . [this] will include activities which are so familiar that their technical character tends to be overlooked, such as the act of writing, using pen and paper.'

Of course, and as the Board of Appeal pointed out, this does not mean that all methods using technical means are patentable. They still have to satisfy the other requirements of novelty, inventive step and being capable of industrial application.

■ Trade marks and the internet

KEY DEFINITION: Use of a sign

Use of a sign for the purposes of trade mark infringement includes using the sign in business papers and in advertising.

Two issues are particularly relevant in terms of the **use of a sign**, being a registered trade mark, on the internet. The first is the use of the trade marks of others as AdWords (advertising keywords used to secure an entry in a sponsored list of hits following the entry of a trade mark in a search engine). The second relates to the use of an advertisement to sell 'grey imports' or 'not-for sale' samples distributed by the trade mark owner. Both types of uses have generated rulings from the Court of Justice of the European Union.

📖 REVISION NOTE

Refer to the form of infringement of a trade mark by using in the course of trade a sign identical to the trade mark in relation to identical goods or services under Article 5(1)(a) of the trade marks Directive, as set out in Chapter 9.

KEY CASE

Case C-329/09 *Interflora Inc.* v *Marks & Spencer plc* [2011] ECR I-08625 CJEU

Concerning: Whether the use of a trade mark as an AdWord without the proprietor's consent infringes that trade mark

Facts

The defendant, not being one of the claimant's network of florists, operated a flower sale and delivery service. It used various terms including the word 'Interflora' as AdWords so that anyone entering 'Interflora' would retrieve amongst the sponsored links list, an advertisement for the defendant.

Legal principle

Using a sign to trigger an advertisement was use of that sign as a trade mark. However, the proprietor was able to prevent such use only if it had an adverse effect on one of the functions of the trade mark, being the essential function of guaranteeing to consumers the origin of the goods or services, the function of guaranteeing the quality of the product or service and the functions of communication, investment and advertising.

In relation to the essential function of guaranteeing the origin of goods or services, that function is adversely affected if the advertisement does not enable reasonably well-informed and reasonably observant internet users, or enables them only with difficulty, to ascertain whether the goods or services referred to by the advertisement originate from the proprietor of the trade mark (or an economically linked undertaking) or, on the contrary, originate from a third party.

Note: in applying this ruling, the High Court held that Marks & Spencer infringed the Interflora trade mark.

The proprietor of a trade mark cannot, on the basis of his trade mark, prevent the further commercialisation of goods placed on the market within the EEA (the EU, Iceland, Liechtenstein and Norway) by the proprietor or with his consent. This doctrine of 'exhaustion of rights' does not apply where those goods have been placed on the market outside the EEA.

KEY STATUTE

Article 7, Directive 2008/95/EC on the approximation of the laws of Member States relating to trade marks (consolidated version)

'Exhaustion of the rights conferred by a trade mark

1 The trade mark shall not entitle the proprietor to prohibit its use in relation to goods which have been put on the market in the Community [now EEA] under that trade mark by the proprietor or with his consent.

2 Paragraph 1 shall not apply where there exist legitimate reasons for the proprietor to oppose further commercialisation of the goods, especially where the condition of the goods is changed or impaired after they have been put on the market.'

This provision applies generally to intellectual property rights and is not limited to trade marks, nor is it limited to online commercialisation but is particularly relevant in that context, given the growth in online sales from traders within the EEA and elsewhere.

KEY CASE

Case C-324/09 *L'Oréal SA* v *eBay International AG* [2011] ECR I-06011, CJEU

Concerning: Whether goods available for sale or via auctions through eBay which had been placed on the market outside the EEA or distributed within the EEA as testers or samples by the trade mark proprietor infringed the trade mark

Facts

L'Oréal and other cosmetics companies complained about goods being sold through eBay via its online auction-style and fixed-price sales. Submitting certain trade marked words to a search engine, such as Google, resulted in a sponsored links list which included links to products available for sale or auction on the eBay site.

Legal principle

1. A private activity, such as a single online sale by an individual is not in the course of trade – however, where a person makes a large quantity of sales though an online marketplace, this goes beyond a private activity and is in the course of trade.

2. Where goods have been placed on the market outside the EEA, sale within the EEA by a third party will infringe.

3. In relation to advertisements for goods placed online, the question of infringement depends on whether those goods are targeted at consumers in a Member State of the EU.

4. By supplying authorised dealers of testers or samples, the trade mark proprietor does not place those testers or samples on the market within the EEA and the doctrine of exhaustion of rights cannot apply to them.

5. The trade mark proprietor can object to the sale of his goods where the packaging containing information such as the identity of the manufacturer or person marketing the goods has been removed where this damages the image of the goods and, consequently, the reputation of the trade mark.

6. Although eBay was using the marks in question, it was not using them in relation to identical goods or services as it was using them to promote its own service of an online marketplace – however, there could still be infringement under Article 5(2) of the trade marks Directive if such use took unfair advantage of or was detrimental to the distinctive character or repute of the trade mark.

7. A service provider, such as eBay, could rely on the 'hosting defence' under Article 14 of the Directive 2000/31/EC on electronic commerce unless it took an active part so as to give it knowledge of any unlawful activity.

! Don't be tempted to . . .

Don't think that simply using another's trade mark in relation to identical or similar goods sold or advertised for sale online infringes, per se. In the context of the internet and use of a trade mark as a keyword or AdWord, the Court of Justice has indicated that one of the functions of a trade mark also must be adversely affected.

✎ EXAM TIP

Make sure you are familiar with Court of Justice cases on the use of trade marks online, such as in AdWords. Demonstrate that you can distinguish between the implications of online use and conventional use of trade marks and to what extent, if any, the principles applicable to the former case might apply to the latter case.

■ Putting it all together

Answer guidelines

See the essay question at the start of the chapter.

Approaching the question

■ Think about the requirements for patentability; consider the test for novelty (the state of the art) and how the state of the art is assessed.

▶

- Reflect on the procedure to obtain a patent, the timescale and cost involved. Note that, whilst a patent gives monopoly protection, patent litigation is notoriously expensive.

Important points to include

- Review the nature of patent rights and the procedure to obtain a patent in the UK, Europe and elsewhere.
- Consider the pros and cons of the patent system.
- Look at the patent system from the perspective of a large multinational company – for example, giving powerful monopoly protection.
- Examine the particular disadvantages of the patent system for SMEs, such as cost, the long time taken before grant, the difficulties in enforcing patents and the vagaries and expense of patent litigation.
- Note that a particular difficulty in the context of computer-implemented inventions is that the state of the art is far from being well-defined unlike some areas such as pharmaceuticals where patent specifications and academic journals provide a fairly accurate picture of the state of the art. This is unlike the software industry which is vast and where only a small proportion of innovations are patented or written up in journals. A patented computer-implemented invention may be attacked on the basis of some obscure or little known software.
- Some patented inventions in the field of software are very wide in scope, particularly in jurisdictions such as the United States and are owned by 'patent trolls' used to threaten software companies. SMEs may be tempted to pay a licence fee rather than risk challenging such patents.
- An SME may find its patents challenged by a large corporation with deep-pockets in a number of different countries, giving potential exposure to immense legal costs.

✓ **Make your answer stand out**

Make suggestions as to how the problems of patenting for SMEs in the software industry could be eased, for example, by adopting a petty patent or utility model scheme as exists in some countries. Also discuss the fact that copyright protection is available but this protection does not prevent third parties writing similar software provided they do not copy the program code or, at least, the architecture or structure of the software at a fairly detailed level.

READ TO IMPRESS

Bakels, R. B. (2009) 'Software patentability: what are the right questions?' 31(10) *EIPR*, 514.

Deschamps, C. (2011) 'Patenting computer-related inventions in the US and in Europe: the need for domestic and international legal harmony' 33(2) *EIPR*, 103

Kemp, R. and Gibbons, C. (2006) 'Database right after *BHB* v *William Hill*: enact and repent at leisure' 22(6) *Computer Law and Security Report*, 493

Kulk, S. (2011) 'Search engines – searching for trouble?' 33(10) *EIPR*, 607

Onslow, R. and Jamal, I. (2013) 'Copyright infringement and software emulation: *SAS Inc* v *World Programming Ltd*' 35(6) *EIPR*, 352

www.pearsoned.co.uk/lawexpress

Go online to access more revision support including quizzes to test your knowledge, sample questions with answer guidelines, podcasts you can download, and more!

And finally, before the exam . . .

Be aware that problem questions on intellectual property are likely to focus on whether the conditions for subsistence or registrability, as appropriate, are satisfied, taking account of any specific exclusions. Ownership and entitlement of rights are also areas that are commonly examined, particularly in situations where the subject-matter has been created by a person who is a self-employed consultant or designer. Issues of infringement and defences usually are tied together. Make sure you know the basic rules on these aspects of intellectual property and are able to apply them to practical situations, making realistic conclusions which are supported by your discussion and arguments.

Essay questions often pick up on difficult and areas of intellectual property law perceived as unsatisfactory, such as the scope of protection for computer programs and pharmaceutical products and the use of trade marks belonging to other undertakings as AdWords. Be prepared to suggest proposal for change, supported by convincing argument, taking all due account of relevant reports, proposals for legislative change and judicial criticism.

Examiners like to keep up to date with the latest developments and may set exam questions based on them, whether a very recent judgment in the Supreme Court or Court of Appeal or a ruling of the Court of Justice of the EU. New and proposed legislation are also examinable. Keep yourself up to date with new developments occurring during the time you take your intellectual property law module and show a keen interest in new and recent developments specifically mentioned by your lecturer.

Finally, plan your revision carefully and cover the entire syllabus unless you have been expressly told something will not be examined. Bear in mind that questions in intellectual property examination papers often cover more than one particular right.

Test yourself

☐ Look at the revision checklists at the start of each chapter. Are you happy that you can now tick them all? If not, go back to the particular chapter and work through the material again. If you are still struggling, seek help from your tutor. ▶

☐ Attempt the sample questions in each chapter and check your answers against the guidelines provided.

☐ Go online to **www.pearsoned.co.uk/lawexpress** for more hands-on revision help and try out these resources:

☐ Try the **test your knowledge** quizzes and see whether you can score full marks for each chapter.

☐ Attempt to answer the **sample questions** for each chapter within the time limit and check your answers against the guidelines provided.

☐ Listen to the **podcast** and then attempt the question it discusses.

☐ **You be the marker** and see whether you can spot the strengths and weaknesses of the sample answers.

☐ Use the **flashcards** to test your recall of the legal principles of the key cases and statutes you've revised and the definitions of important terms.

☐ Make sure you can identify and deal with situations where more than one intellectual property right might be relevant and understand the overlaps and scope of the rights.

☐ Know the rules for subsistence or registration of intellectual property rights and exceptions to those rules.

☐ Be aware that some forms of infringement require copying or other access to the first work and some are monopoly rights, requiring no access to the first work though knowledge may be relevant as regards remedies.

■ Linking it all up

Check where there are overlaps between subject areas. (You may want to review the 'revision note' boxes throughout this text.) Make a careful note of these as knowing how one topic may lead into another can increase your marks significantly. Here are some examples:

✔ There is often an overlap between copyright, especially works of artistic craftsmanship, and design rights.

✔ Privacy and the defence of public interest in relation to copyright and confidential information involve similar issues and may be the subject of an essay question.

✔ The requirement that something must be new and not part of the state of the art in order to be patented requires awareness of confidential information. The need for a non-disclosure agreement before discussing an innovation prior to filing is a necessary part of any advice on patentability.

✔ There may be copyright or design rights in a trade mark. This could be part of a problem question if the artistic work has been commissioned.

✔ Passing off and trade marks are often interchangeable but the law on each is quite different and must be discussed separately.

✔ Computer programs may be protected by both copyright and, in limited situations, patents. You may be asked to discuss which is the more appropriate form of protection or whether a new *sui generis* right should apply to computer programs.

■ Knowing your cases

Make sure you know how to use relevant case law in your answers. Use the table below to focus your revision of the key cases in each topic. To review the details of these cases, refer back to the particular chapter.

Key case	How to use	Related topics
Chapter 1 – Copyright subsistence		
Interlego AG v *Tyco Industries Inc.*	To show the small modifications to a drawing do not give rise to a fresh copyright	Design law, patents law
Walter v *Lane*	The use of skill and judgement in making a shorthand note of an impromptu speech can be the subject of copyright	Originality
Norowzian v *Arks Ltd*	A dramatic work is one which is capable of being performed before a audience	Dramatic work as a film
Hyperion Records Ltd v *Sawkins*	Skill and judgement in 're-creating' an old work in which copyright has expired may bring a new copyright into existence	Originality, musical work
George Hensher Ltd v *Restawhile Upholstery Ltd*	A work of artistic craftsmanship requires some quality, whether it be created by an artist or be the work of a craftsman	Design law

▶

Key case	How to use	Related topics
Chapter 2 – Authorship, ownership and moral rights		
Fisher v *Brooker*	Reworking an existing work may make someone an author or joint author if his input can be regarded as an original contribution to the creation of the work	Originality, joint authorsip
Robin Ray v *Classic FM plc*	Creative contribution is required for joint authorship, not necessarily penmanship	Beneficial ownership and implied licences
Stephenson Jordan & Harrison Ltd v *MacDonald*	Whether an employee is entitled to copyright	Rules as to first ownership of copyright
Blair v *Osborne & Tomkins*	Commissioned works and implied licences	Scope of implied licence
Hyperion Records Ltd v *Sawkins*	Form of acknowledgement of authorship specified by author	Moral right to be identified as author
Confetti Records v *Warner Music UK Ltd*	For a derogatory treatment of a work, it must be prejudicial to the author's honour or reputation	Moral right to object to a derogatory treatment
Chapter 3 – Copyright infringement, remedies and defences		
CBS Songs Ltd v *Amstrad Consumer Electronics plc*	The fact that a copying machine can be used to infringe copyright as well as having legitimate uses does not itself mean that the manufacturer is authorising others to infringe copyright	Copyright infringement by authorisation
Designers Guild Ltd v *Russell Williams Ltd*	The restricted act of copying requires that the defendant has copied a substantial part of the independent skill and labour of the author	Altered copying

Key case	How to use	Related topics
LA Gear Inc. v *Hi-Tec Sports plc*	The test for having reason to believe for secondary infringement of copyright is an objective test, that is, whether a reasonable person having knowledge of the facts known to the defendant would have believed that the item in question was an infringing item	Secondary infringement of copyright
Hyde Park Residence Ltd v *Yelland*	If information contained in a work is published but the information could be published without copying the work, such copying would be outside the public interest defence	Fair dealing

Chapter 4 – Confidentiality

Key case	How to use	Related topics
Coco v *A. N. Clark (Engineers) Ltd*	Sets out a three-step test, being: ■ the information must have the necessary quality of confidence; ■ it must have been imparted in circumstances importing an obligation of confidence ■ there must be an unauthorised use to the detriment of the party communicating the information	Patent law (which may have provided better protection for the moped engine)
Faccenda Chicken Ltd v *Fowler*	Examines the obligation of confidence owed by an ex-employee	Restrictive covenants used to protect an employer's trade secrets
Michael Douglas v *Hello! Ltd (No. 6)*	Use of photographs surreptitiously taken where there was a reasonable expectation of privacy may be a breach of confidence	Commercial confidence
Campbell v *Mirror Group Newspapers*	Use of photographs to reinforce a newspaper article not in the public interest as the news could have been made public without the photographs	Privacy

▶

Key case	How to use	Related topics
Chapter 5 – Patentability, entitlement and ownership		
Lux Traffic Controls Ltd v *Pike Signals Ltd*	An invention is made available to the public by prior use if persons were free in law and equity to examine the invention, whether or not they did so in fact	Novelty
Synthon v *SmithKline Beecham plc (No. 2)*	There is a distinction between disclosure and enablement for the purposes of anticipation	Novelty and trial and error experimentation
Windsurfing International Inc. v *Tabur Marine Ltd*	The four-step test for obviousness restated in Pozzoli and which guards against the danger of using the benefit of hindsight	Inventive step
Conor Medsystems Inc. v *Angiotech Pharmaceuticals Inc.*	There is no requirement that a patent specification should expressly state how an invention works, it being enough if it shows that it is plausible that a particular integer would work	Inventive step and obviousness
Human Genome Sciences Inc. v *Eli Lilly & Co*	The requirement of industrial application can be satisfied if, in the light of the common general knowledge, the invention has a plausible claimed use (note: this principle may not be of universal application)	Industrial application
IDA Ltd v *University of Southampton*	A person who contributes the inventive step is the inventor even if such a person is not skilled in the particular art	Entitlement to a patent
Chapter 6 – Patent infringement, defences and remedies		
Catnic Components Ltd v *Hill & Smith Ltd*	A purposive construction rather than a strict literal interpretation should be applied to patent claims	Scope of patent claims

Key case	How to use	Related topics
Improver Corp v Raymond Industries Ltd	Three-step test for whether a variant infringes a patent, now known as the Protocol questions	Variants
Kirin-Amgen Inc. v Hoechst Marion Roussel Ltd	Applicability of Protocol questions to biotechnologies	Biotech patents
Auchincloss v Agricultural & Veterinary Supplies Ltd	Scope of experimental use	Defence to patent infringement
Schutz (UK) Ltd v Werit UK Ltd	What needs to be considered when deciding if a product has been made or repaired	Repair defence

Chapter 7 – Design law

Key case	How to use	Related topics
Green Lane Products Ltd v PMS International Group Ltd	Indicates that obscure prior art is not taken into account when assessing novelty and is not limited to the type of product for which a design is registered	Whether a design is known to circles specialising in the relevant sector within the Community
PepsiCo Inc v GrupoPromer Mon Graphic SA	Considers the meaning of the 'informed user'	Considering the differences between the design and an earlier design
3M Innovative Properties Co.'s designs	Looks at the exclusion of features dictated by function	Individual character
Samsung Electronics (UK) Ltd v Apple Inc.	It is the design registration that must be compared, not the product itself	Individual character
Procter & Gamble Co. v Reckitt Benckiser (UK) Ltd	Infringement and different overall impression	Design freedom

▶

Key case	How to use	Related topics
Dyson Ltd v *Vax Ltd*	Scope of exclusion for design dictated by function	Functional and aesthetic considerations
Fundación Española para la Innovación de la Artesanía (FEIA) v *Cul de Sac EspacioCreativo SL*	Design created under a commission belongs to the designer	First ownership of Community design
Dyson Ltd v *Qualtex (UK) Ltd*	Guidance on exclusions to the UK unregistered design	'Must-fit', 'must-match' and surface decoration

Chapter 8 – Trade marks registrability

Shield Mark BV v *Joost Kist*	For a sign to be capable of graphical representation, it must be clear, precise, self-contained, easily accessible, intelligible, durable and objective	Registering sounds as trade marks
Windsurfing Chiemsee Productions v *Huber and Attenberger*	Geographical names, despite the general exclusion, may be registered on the basis of acquired distinctiveness	Absolute grounds for refusal of registration
Koninklijke Philips Electronics v *Remington Consumer Products Ltd*	Shapes necessary to obtain a technical effect are unregistrable even if there are other shapes that can achieve that technical effect	The registrability of shape marks
Lloyd Schuhfabrik Meyer & Co. GmbH v *Klisjen Handel BV*	The likelihood of confusion is more likely the more distinctive the earlier trade mark is and the more similar the goods or services for which the earlier trade mark is registered compared with those for which the sign in question is to be used	Likelihood of confusion on the part of the public

Key case	How to use	Related topics
General Motors v *Yplon*	Whether a trade mark has established a reputation in the eyes of a substantial part of the relevant public depends on factors such as market share, intensity of sale, geographical location, duration of use and advertising	Refusal of registration where use of the sign would take unfair advantage of or be detrimental to a trade mark having a reputation

Chapter 9 – Trade mark infringement

Key case	How to use	Related topics
Arsenal Football Club plc v *Matthew Reed (Court of Justice ruling)*	Unchecked use of a trade mark by another trader, for example, as a badge of allegiance, could adversely affect its function as an indication of origin	Passing off
LTJ Diffusion SA v *Sadas Vertbaudet SA*	A sign may be identical to a trade mark if it contains all the elements of the trade mark or, when viewed as a whole, contains insignificant differences unlikely to be noticed by the average consumer	Identical marks
L'Oréal SA v *Bellure NV*	The proprietor of a trade mark may prevent comparative advertising using his trade mark where this does not fall within that permitted under the misleading advertising Directive	Comparative advertising
Asprey and Garrard Ltd v *WRA (Guns) Ltd*	The own name defence does not extent to the use of one's own name for a newly-formed company or as new trade names	Own-name defence
Bravado Merchandising Services Ltd v *Mainstream Publishing (Edinburgh) Ltd*	Purely descriptive use does not infringe, for example, where a trade mark name is used to describe the characteristics of goods, rather than being used in a trade mark sense	Descriptive names

▶

Key case	How to use	Related topics
Gillette Company v *LA-Laboratories Ltd*	Using a trade mark if necessary to indicate the intended purpose of goods, for example, as accessories, if in accordance with honest practices	Defences and honest practices
L'Oreal (UK) Ltd v *Johnson & Johnson*	Whether a communication amounts to an actionable threat is a question of how it would be understood by the ordinary recipient in the position of the claimant	Groundless threats

Chapter 10 – Passing off

Key case	How to use	Related topics
Reckitt & Colman Products Ltd v *Borden Inc.*	Sets out the 'classic trinity' for a passing off action, being: goodwill, misrepresentation and damage	Basic requirements for passing off
Erven Warnink Besloten Vennootschap v *J Townend & Sons Ltd*	Damage to reputation can be sufficient for passing off	Ownership of goodwill in a name by several traders
Scandecor Development AB v *Scandecor Marketing AB*	Goodwill is associated with the company actually doing trade in the UK	Ownership of goodwill
Arsenal Football Club plc v *Reed*	Customers or ultimate consumers may be deceived. A disclaimer may negate misrepresentation for passing off	Trade mark infringement
Taittinger SA v *Allbev Ltd*	Erosion of distinctiveness of a name in which goodwill exists may be relevant damage for passing off even in the absence of proof of consumers being deceived	Damage for passing off (cf trade mark law and damage to a trade mark with a reputation)
Irvine v *Talksport Ltd*	Misrepresentation may extend to falsely suggesting endorsement by a celebrity	Common field of activity

Key case	How to use	Related topics
Bristol Conservatories Ltd v *Conservatories Custom Built Ltd*	Claiming another trader's goods or services as one's own is an actionable misrepresentation	Inverse passing off
Bostick Ltd v *Sellotape GB Ltd*	A misrepresentation which occurs only after sale is not actionable as passing off	Post-sale confusion
Marks & Spencer plc v *One in a Million Ltd*	Registering the name of another trader's company as a domain name is passing off. The domain name is an instrument of fraud	Cybersquatting

Chapter 11 – Intellectual property, computer software and the internet

SAS Institute Inc. v *World Programming Ltd*	Emulating the functions and operation of a computer program without copying its actual code or detailed architecture, there is no infringement of copyright	Non-textual copying
Football Dataco Ltd v *Stan James (Abingdon) Ltd*	Whether the labour and skill used in creating data to be included in a database is sufficient for copyright subsistence	Copyright in a database
British Horseracing Board Ltd v *William Hill Organisation Ltd*	The act of creating data does not fall within the meaning of obtaining	Database right
Aerotel/ Macrossan Patent Application	Sets out a test for determining whether the exclusion of computer programs or business methods, as such, applies	Exclusions from the meaning of 'invention' in the UK
Hitachi/Auction method	Anything performed by a programmed computer, whether claimed as an entity or the activity in question, has a technical character and is not excluded	Exclusions from the meaning of 'invention' at the EPO (contrast with above case)

▶

Key case	How to use	Related topics
Interflora Inc. v *Marks & Spencer plc*	Using another's trade mark as an AdWord does not infringe if the functions of the trade mark are not adversely affected	Trade mark infringement
L'Oréal SA v *eBay International AG*	Considers some of the circumstances under which a trade mark proprietor can object to the further commercialisation of his goods in the context of the internet	Exhaustion of rights

■ Sample question

Below is a problem question that incorporates overlapping areas of the law. See whether you can answer this question drawing upon your knowledge of the whole subject area. Guidelines on answering this question are included at the end of this section.

PROBLEM QUESTION

Imagine that you are sitting in the first-class cabin of a newly designed aircraft on a flight to New York. You are watching an in-flight movie which is a remake of an old classic. You have the well-known WHOOSH drink in your hand. This is contained in a new and unusually shaped plastic bottle with a label containing a striking image and the word 'whoosh'. During the flight you read the free in-flight magazine, *GO*. Your seat is like no other aircraft seat you have ever seen. It has a novel reclining mechanism, converting into a bed and it is apparently the safest seat available as it is highly energy absorbing.

You booked your ticket online with DANAIR but noticed when you entered a search for DANAIR, the first website in the list of hits was JETAWAY, a rival airline. DANAIR is a registered trade mark.

Discuss, using relevant statutory and case law, the intellectual property rights that you may have encountered on your journey.

Answer guidelines

Approaching the question

First make a plan. Make sure that you identify as many relevant IP rights as possible. You will get more marks for addressing *all* of the issues adequately than one or two of the issues very well. You want your reader to understand that you have a solid understanding of intellectual property rights.

Important points to include

- The aircraft is newly designed so there may be many design rights here. The look of aspects of the aircraft may be protected. There may be Community design rights (registered and unregistered) and UK registered designs. You should explain about novelty and individual character, products, complex products, and the exceptions. Apart from design rights in the overall appearance of the aircraft, they are likely to exist in many other products, such as aspects of the cabin design, the crew uniforms and even the trays and utensils used for meals. Don't forget to mention the UK unregistered design right which can apply to functional designs (shape or configuration) providing they are original and not commonplace.

- There are almost certainly many patent rights in the aircraft, for example, in the mechanical, electrical and electronic equipment, instrumentation and the flight control systems. Mention the basic requirements under section 1 of the Patents Act 1977. There may also be rights in relation to software used in the aircraft, such as computer programs and databases, providing they are the author's own intellectual creation. Database right may subsist in, for example, collections of data relating to airports, such as approach paths, runway, taxiway and terminal buildings, provided the data were existing data collected during the making of the relevant databases (*British Horseracing Board* v *William Hill*) and providing they are the result of a relevant substantial investment. Copyright and database rights are also likely to exist in the airline booking systems. Mention that computer programs fall within the exceptions to patent protection under section 1(2) of the Patents Act 1977 but may be protected if there is a technical effect (*Hitachi*, cf. *Aerotel and Macrossan*).

- Your in-flight movie is likely to have copyright protection. However, it is a remake, so explain originality. If only an idea is taken, and a film is remade, there is no infringement of the original film itself (*Norowzian* v *Arks*). You should also point out that the soundtrack is part of the film.

- The name of your drink could be a registered or unregistered trade mark. It is a well-known brand so there is potential for goodwill to exist for the purposes of passing off. The name WOOOSH would certainly pass the first hurdle for ▶

registration for Article 3 of the trade marks Directive (s. 3 of the Act) as it is not descriptive or laudatory (providing there is no conflict under the relative grounds for refusal). As the brand is well known it may have reached the status of a mark with a reputation for Article 4(3) of the Directive (s. 5(3) of the Act). To determine this you should discuss *General Motors* v *Yplon*.

- The shape of the WHOOSH bottle is not a sculpture for copyright purposes (*Lucasfilm* v *Ainsworth*) but the image could be a work of artistic copyright providing it is original in the copyright sense.

- The magazine will have copyright in the articles and the photographs and a separate copyright in its typographical arrangement. There will be no copyright in the name of the magazine, as names are not regarded as literary works as, generally, they lack originality.

- A number of aspects of the chair could be patented, such as the reclining mechanism and the safety features, so you should discuss the criteria for patentability. Apart from novelty, inventive step could be an issue. There may also be design rights (registered and unregistered) available for the appearance, shape or configuration of the chair.

- As JETAWAY came top in the list of hits retrieved by the search engine, it is possible that JETAWAY has used DANAIR as an AdWord, as in *Interflora* v *Marks & Spencer*. You should discuss the CJEU ruling in that case and whether such use of another's trade mark infringes the DANAIR trade mark.

✓ **Make your answer stand out**

This is an international flight. Point out that not all these rights may be registered in the UK or, in the case of passing off, have goodwill in the UK. Show that you understand that intellectual property rights are territorial in nature.

Glossary of terms

The glossary is divided into two parts: key definitions and other useful terms. The key definitions can be found within the chapter in which they occur as well as in the glossary below. These definitions are the essential terms that you must know and understand in order to prepare for an exam. The additional list of terms provides further definitions of useful terms and phrases which will also help you answer examination and coursework questions effectively. These terms are highlighted in the text as they occur but the definition can only be found here.

■ Key definitions

Authorise	In relation to copyright infringement, authorise means to grant or purport to grant to a third person the right to do the act complained of.
Average consumer	The average consumer is taken to be a consumer of the goods concerned who is reasonably well informed, reasonably observant and circumspect (careful).
Bad faith	Bad faith is behaviour falling short of acceptable standards of commercial behaviour. It must be assessed objectively and case by case.
Commonplace	The word 'commonplace' was new to English law when introduced by Directive 87/54/EEC protecting semiconductor topographies. There are a number of judicial statements, none of which are entirely satisfactory. They include: '. . . any design which is trite, trivial, common-or-garden, hackneyed or of the type which would excite no peculiar attention in those in the relevant art is likely to be commonplace' 'What really matters is what prior designs the experts are able to identify and how much those designs are shown to be current in the thinking of designers in the field at the time of creation of the design in question'.

It is important to note, however, that a design which has become very familiar does not necessarily become 'commonplace'. For example, if a design is applied to an article made by one manufacturer which sells in large numbers, that does not necessarily mean it is commonplace.

Community design
A community design has a unitary character and has equal effect throughout the Community. It may only be registered, transferred, surrendered, declared invalid or its use prohibited in relation to the entire Community (now EU).

Comparative advertising
Comparative advertising is the use of a competitor's trade mark to highlight the comparative advantage of one's own rival goods or services.

Database
A database is a collection of independent works, data or other materials which are arranged in a systematic or methodical way and are individually accessible by electronic or other means.

Descriptive mark
A descriptive mark describes the goods or services in question and so cannot distinguish the goods or services of one undertaking from those of other undertakings, for it is applicable to all such goods.

Distinctive mark
A mark that is distinctive is capable of distinguishing the goods or services of one undertaking from those of other undertakings.

Goodwill
Goodwill is the attractive force attached to the name, get-up or logo which brings in custom.

Groundless threats
No matter how ambiguous or indecisive, a communication will be regarded as a threat if understood by the ordinary recipient of the communication to be a threat to bring infringement proceedings.

Identical marks (when trade marks are identical)
The average, reasonably well informed, observant and circumspect customer assessing the mark globally may not notice the addition of a hyphen or an apostrophe, especially when they are apart, but would notice the inclusion of an extra word, if the word would not go unnoticed by the average consumer.

Injunction
An injunction is an order of the court which prohibits an act or the commencement or continuance of an act. Alternatively, an injunction might order a person to perform some act.

Inverse passing off
This is where the defendant falsely claims that the claimant's goods or services are actually made or provided by the defendant.

Joint authorship
A work of joint authorship is where the contribution of each author cannot be separated, whereas the contribution of each

author in a work of co-authorship is distinct, discrete and separately distinguishable.

Misrepresentation A false description made consciously or unconsciously by the defendant. Such representation can be implied by the use of a mark, trade name or get-up with which the goods of the claimant are associated in the minds of a substantial number of ordinary, sensible members of the public who have been or are likely to be misled due to the representation.

Original A work is original for copyright purposes if it has originated from the author and has not been copied from another work. For computer programs and copyright databases, a work is original if it is the author's own intellectual creation.

Passing off Passing off is an attempt by trader B to take advantage of the goodwill established by trader A, to the detriment of trader A.

Patent infringement Infringement of a UK patent occurs if a validly patented product or process is exploited within the UK without the patentee's consent in the absence of a valid defence.

Person skilled in the art See **Skilled person**

Post-sale confusion Post-sale confusion is where the misrepresentation comes after the goods have been purchased.

Private information Information or conduct, the disclosure of which would be highly offensive to a reasonable person of ordinary sensibilities.

Purposive approach The purposive approach looks at the purpose or reason for making the claim.

Similar goods or services Goods or services are similar if they are in competition; if the consumer would buy one instead of the other.

Skilled person An unimaginative person, or team of uninventive people, with the common general knowledge available to a person in the field at the date of filing. They will only think the obvious and will not question general assumptions.

Trade mark – basic requirements for registration A mark will only be registered as a trade mark if it is a sign, if it can be represented graphically and if it is capable of distinguishing one trader's goods or services from those of another.

Trade secret A trade secret is information that would cause real harm if it were disclosed to a competitor and the owner had limited dissemination of the information.

Use of a sign Use of a sign for the purposes of trade mark infringement includes using the sign in business papers and in advertising.

■ Other useful terms

Artists' resale right	The right of an author of an artistic work or manuscript to a royalty on subsequent public resale of his work.
Assignment	Transfer of ownership of an intellectual property right, such as copyright or a patent.
Author	Generally, for the original works of copyright, the author is the person who creates the work.
Beneficial ownership	This applies typically to overcome a failure to properly provide for ownership, for example, by means of an express assignment of a right, so that the person who has paid for the creation of the work in question is given the equitable right to use it, notwithstanding that the creater remains the owner at law.
Community trade mark	A Community trade mark has a unitary character and has equal effect throughout the Community. It may only be registered, transferred, surrendered, revoked or declared invalid or its use prohibited in relation to the entire Community (now EU).
European Economic Area (EEA)	The Member States of the European Union, Iceland, Liechtenstein and Norway.
Exhaustion of rights	The doctrine of exhaustion of rights prevents the owner of an intellectual property right exercising that right to prevent the subsequent commercialisation of goods placed on the market with the EEA by him or with his consent.
Filing date	The date of filing an application for a formal intellectual property right, such as a patent. There is a period of time after the first filing of an application during which the novelty of applications filed elsewhere will be determined on the basis of the state of the art at the time of the first filing. For patents, this period is 12 months. For registered designs it is six months (this applies both to novelty and individual character).
Individual character	A design has individual character if the overall impression it produces on an *informed user* differs from the overall impression produced on such a user by any design which has been made available to the public.
Informed user	The '*informed user*' is not the same as the '*average consumer*' of trade mark law. The informed user has experience of similar products and will be reasonably discriminatory and able to appreciate sufficient detail to decide whether or not the design under consideration creates a different overall impression. The degree of design freedom is taken into account.

Permitted acts

These are acts expressly permitted under the Copyright, Designs and Patents Act 1988 which would otherwise infringe copyright.

Priority date

The date of filing a patent application. Where an earlier application for the same invention is made elsewhere in the previous 12 months and the priority of that earlier application is claimed in the later filing, that earlier filing date is the priority date.

Royalty

A payment mechanism to allow another person to exploit an intellectual property right under a licence agreement or assignment, normally calculated as a percentage of the income derived from sales of works, products or articles subject to the right.

State of the art

In relation to an invention, it means all matter made available to the public at the priority date by means of a written or oral description, by use or in any other way, whether in the UK or elsewhere.

Index